The Book of Pall Mall

How the body should be turned from the waist upwards
in making the stroke. The game of pall mall

J. M. SCOTT

THE
BOOK OF PALL MALL

HEINEMANN : LONDON

William Heinemann Ltd

LONDON MELBOURNE TORONTO

CAPE TOWN AUCKLAND

First published 1965
© by J. M. Scott 1965

Printed in England by Alabaster Passmore and Sons Ltd,
London and Maidstone

Foreword

NEVER HAVE I enjoyed writing a book so much as this one, though I have written more than I care to remember. I undertook it almost casually. I thought I knew Pall Mall well enough, having been a member of one of its clubs for a quarter of a century. My only concern was that I might not find enough to say about it.

I started working, and received a shock. I found that I did not know why Pall Mall was so named, when it became a street or in what circumstances. More important, although I knew its stones, bricks and concrete by sight, they were connected with the names of no more than two or three architects; and an architect is only the instrument, not the originator of an idea. The history of the street was a blank in my mind of which I was not even conscious. I never wondered when I went into a club or shop or saw a building being demolished what had stood on that spot or who had lived, worked or recreated himself there in the past. Take one example. I had seen over a door of Schomberg House a blue plaque recording that Gainsborough was there nearly two hundred years ago. But what hint does that give of the rich and varied history of that single building?

Country paths and lanes have always fascinated me. Their primary purpose, presumably, was to get from one place to another. So why do they wander as they do? Their line was governed by many factors – safety, better going, vegetation, private ownerships, a place at which to rest and water the horses. Pall Mall did not originate like that, yet it is what it is as the result of the choice of alternatives by thirty generations. It is the people that matter. Therefore I set about disinterring them, mainly at the British Museum, Cambridge University Library and the London Library, and by talking or writing to knowledgeable people. Therein lay the fascination, in trying to bring Pall Mall back to continuous life. Whenever I felt I was succeeding, even to the small degree I may have achieved, I was happy as a magician. What greater possible pleasure is there than bringing back to life?

If it be said that this book is anecdotal I accept the charge. Small incidents are the molecules of history, more important than the big decisions and actions of the history books because they in their multitude brought the latter about. My only concern was to select wisely and condense severely enough to get it all within the covers of a single volume which would not be too heavy in any sense. It is a great disservice to history to make reading it a labour. And I have wanted to show gratitude. I have wanted like a guest at a party to give all I could in return.

I am grateful to Rothmans of Pall Mall for putting forward the idea of this book, and for insisting that the part played by their founder should not occupy more space than its general interest justified. I am grateful to my publishers for suggesting me as author instead of someone better qualified. One would have thought they would have wanted a person who knew something about the subject. Since I did not I am grateful to those who educated me, mainly authors ranging in time from the earliest days of Pall Mall to the present, some anonymous, still more virtually forgotten, a few well known. My biggest single debt is to those responsible for the *Survey of London*, Vols. XXIX and XXX. Most of my architectural facts are thence derived. This enormous and magnificent work is by far the greatest authority on the building and development of the Parish. But it contains besides paragraphs, sentences or – even more important – references concerning *people*, which set me digging in fruitful places not only, as it proved, to unearth a particular story but to give me a clue to others as interesting.

The principal books which I have consulted are listed in the Bibliography; and sources of particular value are, I hope, always acknowledged in the text as well.

It is, I repeat, in a spirit of gratitude for privileged pleasure that I offer the chapters which follow.

J. M. SCOTT

Contents

Illustrations

Acknowledgements

Acknowledgements are due to the following for permission to reproduce the plates indicated:

British Museum – Frontispiece and plate 15; John R. Freeman & Co – plates 18 and 20; Martin Koretz – plate 24; National Portrait Gallery for the pictures of Gainsborough, Reynolds, and Lord Lyttleton – plate 9; R. B. Fleming & Co Ltd – plate 7; Radio Times Hulton Picture Library – plates 6, 14, 22, and 23a; Royal Academy of Arts – plate 8; The Wallace Collection – plate 10; plate 16 is Crown Copyright reserved.

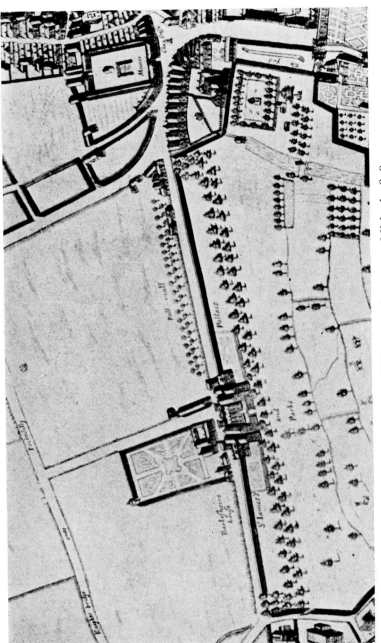

1   Faithorne and Newcourt's map, published 1658

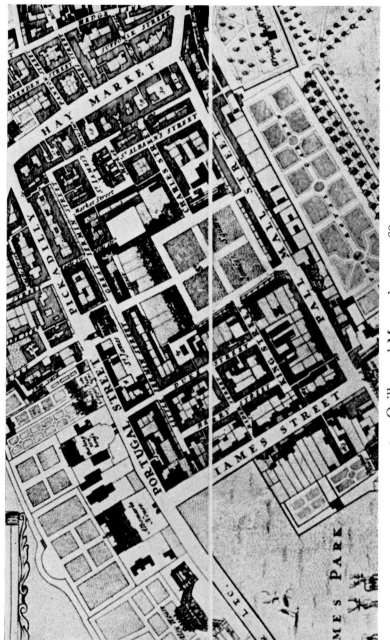

2   Ogilby and Morgan's map, 1681–2

I
What's in a Name?

IN THE YEAR 1660 the street called Pall Mall was a pall mall alley. The word 'alley' signified a strip of land, lined by trees, not a narrow street between houses. There were practically no buildings in the area except for St James's Palace, which Henry VIII had built on the site of the five-hundred-year-old hospital for leprous maidens. What is now St James's Park had then no lake, but had been enclosed for the use of the palace. The quadrilateral to the north of this, bounded by the Haymarket, Piccadilly, and St James's Street, was known as St James's Field. Most of the few buildings in this field had been pulled down on the order of Charles I, so the picture we start with is of park land and fields.

A main road ran across this sward. It was the continuation of the Strand, a highway dating back at least to Norman times. From Charing Cross it followed the line of Warwick House Street (there was, of course, no Trafalgar Square) and ran between the pall mall alley and the wall of St James's Park to St James's Palace. Beyond the palace it followed the present Cleveland Row, crossed the fields (which became the Green Park) to reach Hyde Park Corner, and continued to the westward. Thus the pall mall alley lay between this highway and St James's Field. This smooth ride lined by elm trees was used partly as a promenade but mainly as a playing field. For pall mall was a game. It had originated in Italy in the Middle Ages. It is referred to in a Florentine carnival song printed about 1500 – 'giocator di palla a maglio' – player of ball-to-mallet. It is a nice thought that Italians were enjoying this game before the Renaissance set them to building palaces which two or three centuries later were to be the architectural models, or at least the inspiration, of Pall Mall clubs. The game which gave its name to the street had by then become extinct. It deserves to be reconstructed here.

From Italy palla a maglio travelled to France in the early sixteenth century. There it was generally called *paille maile* or *mail,* and was considerably developed. Joseph Lautier, who published *Nouveaux Règles pour le Jeu de Mail* in 1717, mentions four forms of the game – *au rouet,* singles; *au partie,* two or more players on each side; *aux grands coups,* long driving; *à la chicane,* in open country. The first three were played on a smooth prepared alley several hundred yards long and lined by 'well jointed staves or moderately thick planks of oak'. The purpose of this barrier, the *tambour,* was to contain the ball. A relatively small alley was advised for country houses, 150–200 paces long and ten or twelve across. The fixtures were either an iron peg at each end or a hoop (sometimes a ring on the end of a spike) at each end and an iron peg in the middle. The ball had to be played from one peg to hit the other, or through the further hoop and back to the central peg, in both cases in fewer strokes than one's opponent – except for the long driving contests in which one merely hit the ball as far as possible. Four hundred and five paces is described as a good drive, as indeed it sounds. In the minimum strokes game, going out of bounds – over the tambour – cost two strokes.

Balls were made of boxwood, and were about two-and-a-half inches in diameter. The size was not fixed by the rules. In fact players were advised to use small balls on wet, sticky ground and larger, heavy ones in dry and fast conditions. Much depended on the skill of the ball maker. One ball became so famous that it was given a name, *la Bernarde.* It could always be driven farther than any other. The mallets were something like croquet mallets but very much lighter, more like polo sticks. (There is a pair in the British Museum.) The striking faces were hooped with iron and set back at a slight angle to loft the ball.

The fourth form of the game, *à la chicane,* was very similar to golf, as the following quotations show: 'It is played in open country, in avenues, roads, and any place where people are wont to meet: the first stroke is usually a tee shot, after which the ball must be played wherever it lies, however stony and difficult its position. [It is however stated elsewhere that 'if a ball breaks to pieces the player may use another'.] The match is finished when the ball strikes a particular tree or a marked stone serving as a goal. To avoid injuring those in front, an interval of at least a hundred paces should be allowed, and a player should always cry "Fore" before playing. In the tee-shot the ball may be teed on sand, small stones, a rolled-up card or piece of wood.'

If 'club' were substituted for 'mallet' in the following instructions, they might well apply to golf: 'The mallet must not be swung too quickly, but evenly and under complete control; it should pause an instant at the top of the swing in order to deliver the blow with vigour, bringing into play the strength of the wrists, without however altering the position of the body, arms, and legs, so as not to disturb the aim taken when the eye was fixed upon the ball.'

But pall mall was not golf, or even an early form of it; merely a similar game. An English writer in the days of James I describes golf as 'an ancient game of Scotland not unlike palemaille.' And in the Book of Articles which accused Mary, Queen of Scots, of complicity in the murder of her unsatisfactory husband it is stated that soon after Darnley's death she was seen at Seton with her favourite, Bothwell, playing 'one day richt oppinlie at the fieldis with the pal mall and goif'. Very possibly Mary, who had been educated in France, introduced pall mall to Scotland. Her son, James VI of Scotland, brought it to England when he became James I of the United Kingdom. Certainly it was in the class of royal games. 'Jeu de Mail' carried this sonorously warning introduction:

'Louis, by the grace of God, King of France and Navarre. To our well beloved trusty Councillors, Members of our Court of Parliament, etc. . . .

'We forbid all printers, booksellers, and other persons, of what quality and condition soever, to print or cause to be printed or copied, to sell or retail the said "New Rules of the Game of Mail" and to make any extract thereof for whatever reason, even from a foreign impression, without the written consent of the petitioner or his assigns, under penalty of a fine of 500 francs for each offence, to be proportioned one third to us . . . '

It was an elegant game. Lautier says: 'It is undoubted that of all the many games the game of Mail is the most pleasant, the least tiring, and the best for health; it is not violent; one may play, converse, and take a walk in good company – all at the same time.' Sir Robert Dollington, who saw the game before it reached England, wrote: 'Among all the exercises of France, I prefer none before the Palle-maille, both because it is a Gentleman-like sport, not violent, and yields good occasion and opportunity of discourse, as they walke from the one marker to the other.' James I, having brought it to England, advised his son Henry – 'The exercises that I would have you use (although but moderatlie, not making a craft of them) are running, leaping, wrestling, fencing, dauncing, and playing at the caitche or tennise, archery, pall maille, and such like other faire and pleasant field games.'

The only person to suggest any violence or aggressiveness in the game is the obsequious Waller. Referring to Charles II he writes:

Here a well-polished Mall gives us the joy
To see our Prince his matchless force imploy;
No sooner has he toucht the flying ball,
But 'tis already more than half the mall,
And such a fury from his arm has got
As from a smoking Culverin 'twere shot.

May that ill fate my enemies befall
To stand before his anger or his ball.

Naturally, the game had to be played with a proper respect for appearances. The ruling in *Jeu de Mail* is: 'It is not pleasant to see persons of quality playing in public without a jacket or waistcoat, or without a wig', and: 'It must not be forgotten that gloves should always be worn, which, besides being tidy, help to keep the mallet firmly in the hand . . . and protect the hand from blisters.' And also: 'He [the player] must take his aim with arms and eye without much ado or grimace.'

It is remarkable that a game so much enjoyed and respected by people of quality should have disappeared completely. Presumably golf and croquet drew away those who enjoyed hitting balls about in a gentlemanlike manner. There is no record of how many malls there were in Europe at the peak of the game's popularity, but in the reign of Charles II there were still three in Paris – at the Tuileries, Palais Royal and Arsenal. There was a well-shaded one at Blois. That at Tours was spoken of as the noblest of all, having seven rows of tall elms. There was one at Lyons. In Switzerland there was one at Geneva, and in Germany at Altona. Yet only London's Pall Mall is remembered by its name.

Its pronunciation has always been something of a social shibboleth. The first syllables of the Italian *palla maglio* could only rhyme with 'Hal'. The French *paille maile* or *mail* suggest comparison with 'hail'. But since we call Firenze Florence, and pronounce Paris quite differently from the French, there is no reason to be bound by foreign precedents, even from older sources. The pall mall played by Mary Queen of Scots would rhyme with 'Hal', but, possibly, if the *a* was of the broad Scots type, with 'awl'. James I's pall maille strongly suggests that the two words did not rhyme with each other. Peter Mundy, the diarist and traveller, a completely uninhibited but generally phonetic speller, has 'palle malle', which suggests that the two words did rhyme and that the *a* was short. But in a survey made

5

in 1650 the Commissioners for Crown Lands refer to 140 elm trees 'standinge in Pall Mall walke in a very decent and Regular manner'. And in a reference to the game by Pepys in the reign of Charles II, the alley's name is transcribed Pell Mell. Researching in historical sequence we appear to be getting somewhere. But the first dictionary-type ruling is in Blount's *Glossographia,* published in 1670: '. . . this game was heretofore used in the long alley near St James's and vulgarly called Pell-Mell'.

Having thus established that the name can be pronounced however we like, in every case with justification, we can turn to its application to a street. There would appear to have been no good reason to make the alley into a road, for one parallel and near to it already existed – the ancient highway already mentioned. The explanation is to be found in the character of Charles II.

It is understandable, if not excusable, that Charles felt little sense of duty towards his country. He had returned after his father had been beheaded, only to be defeated at Worcester and hounded from place to place for six weeks with a price on his head before he again escaped to France. Then, France and England becoming better friends, he had been forced to wander from land to land. Called to the throne at last at the age of thirty, he landed in Dover with two ideas firmly in his head: nothing should send him wandering again and nobody should interfere with his personal pleasures. One of his first pre-occupations was to improve the royal park of St James. It was planted with fruit trees and ornamental shrubs, and stocked with deer. A 'canal' was made, the original of the present lake. Here Charles could fish, feed the ducks and exercise his spaniels. Also a new mall was laid out, just inside the northern wall of the park, as close to the south side of the ancient highway as the old mall was to the north of it.

Waller was soon spinning silken couplets about these improvements:

. . . 'tis of more renown

To make a river than to build a town.

And, prophetically –

Methinks I see the love that shall be made,

The lovers walking in the amorous shade,

The Gallants dancing at the River's side.

They bath in summer and in winter slide.

The new alley was the 'well polisht mall' already referred to. Pepys discovered a couple of years later how it had been made. 'I walked in the park, discoursing with the Keeper of the Pell Mell, who was sweeping of it, who told me of what the earth is mixed that do make the floor of the Mall, and that overall there is cockleshells, powdered and spread to keep it fast; which however in dry weather turns to dust and deadens the ball.'

Evidently a great deal of trouble and money was expended on the new mall. But, quite apart from its own dust, clouds stirred up by carriages on the old highway blew over the wall and were 'very troublesome to the players at Mall'. It must have been just as troublesome to the players on the old alley, but that was not in a royal park. Now the nuisance had to be stopped, even though it meant closing a highroad which had been used by the public since the year 1200 at least. So in July 1661 the old highway was blocked off by a fence and a new road opened in its place along the old pall mall alley.

It may be inferred that the actual work of roadmaking was minimal: the alley surface would do for a start. Not until it had been in use as a road for a year was Pall Mall paved. Its eastern end was connected with the Strand, but its western stopped short of the Green Park (so called after 1668) instead of continuing to Hyde Park Corner, Colnbrook and Reading, as the ancient highway had done. Here and there in St James's Field there was a certain amount of building on sites which had been acquired before the Civil War. But beside the new street there were no houses except for St James's Palace, the tennis court

7

and the Physic Garden at the western end, and at the eastern a small group of buildings which had faced onto the ancient highway and therefore had their backs to Pall Mall. The new street was named Catherine Street after Charles's queen, Catherine of Braganza. But this the conservative Londoners ignored. They continued to call it the Pall Mall.

2

The Aristocratic Faubourg

IF IT NEEDS an effort of the imagination to picture the present-day parish of St James's south of Piccadilly as the open field it was three centuries ago, how much more so to have foreseen it then as it is now. The lay-out was planned very much as it is now as soon as the pall mall alley was made into a street. That conversion may well have been the inspiration of the idea: certainly it made it possible. Drawings were submitted for the development of St James's Field with a central piazza (St James's Square) framed by a quadrilateral of outlying streets – St James's Street, Piccadilly, Haymarket and Pall Mall. The street plan was in almost all essentials the same as it is today. With Ogilby and Morgan's map, printed about 1682 and therefore recording the first twenty years of development – unless you happened to be in search of Regent Street or Waterloo Place – you could find your way about well enough.

Pall Mall street was not in itself a practical conception. It was born overnight at the whim of a king without proving its usefulness by going through the usual evolution of track, path, lane, road. Unlike the ancient highway which it superseded it was almost valueless as a means of communication, the prime purpose of any street. Neither end was clear, the eastern being restricted by a narrow connexion with the Strand; the western obstructed until 1679 by the old tennis court buildings adjoining St James's Palace, with the boundary of the present Green Park a hundred paces beyond. But in this case difficulty of entrance and exit was no disadvantage: it was intentional. The Field was to become an island of aristocracy. It was to be self-sufficient, residential, inward-looking. It was to be disturbed by no thoroughfare. Conveniently close to the royal palaces and the seat of government, it was to be the domestic retreat of courtiers, parliamentarians and foreign embassies. Further inspection of Ogilby and Morgan's map will bring out this intention to keep the area discreetly aloof from the ordinary course of London life. Modern alterations have opened it up to a certain extent; but it is still remarkably self-contained.

The heart of this royal *faubourg* was to be St James's Square. First referred to as the Piazza, then called the Place Royale, it soon acquired its present name. Here the finest houses of all were to be built for the noblest in the land, including royalty. The streets framing it would be subtly less aristocratic. Sutton Nicholls' view of the square in 1727 shows the execution, not the plan, from which it differs in at least one interesting point. But more clearly than any map it brings out the character of the houses. Those on the square are noticeably grander than those of the surrounding streets. They all look inwards, the Piccadilly buildings (on the horizon) included. The parish church, essential to a residential area, opens on Jermyn Street, turning its back on the mere bordering street of Piccadilly. The equally essential market is out of sight on the right, sufficiently removed from the aristocratic centre. The artist is, of course, looking from Pall Mall.

The man who thought out this building plan, and who was ingeniously, diplomatically, obstinately putting it into effect until his death, was Henry Jermyn, Earl of St Albans. St James's was his brain child, a thing born not of male and female but of character and experience. Jermyn's life is therefore germane to this story. Knowing his name so well from a street of his planning (all the streets of St James's are named after royalty or members of the St Albans family, with the exception of egregious Pall Mall); knowing the result of his planning, one unconsciously forms a mental picture of the man. It may be interesting to compare this picture with the biographical sketch which follows.

As the second son of a knight Jermyn had no particular advantage at birth, but his first appointment was not without opportunity, for in 1624 he was posted as gentleman in attendance to the Embassy at Paris. He took to diplomacy like a cat to cream, and Paris – the handsomest and best laid-out of cities, at least in the seventeenth century – undoubtedly captured his imagination.

In 1628 he was appointed vice-Chamberlain to Queen Henrietta Maria. It was frequently said, and not only by his enemies, that his success thereafter depended on his skill in the courtly arts, and the consequent favour of the Queen. Five years later, when Lord Holland challenged Lord Weston in a quarrel which concerned the Queen, Jermyn carried the challenge – and served a period of imprisonment as a result. In the same year he was in trouble of a different kind. He seduced Eleanor Villiers, one of the Queen's Maids of Honour, and refused to marry her. But curiously – so, at any rate, it seems to a man – the Queen was not annoyed. She appointed Jermyn her Master of the Horse.

In the reign of Charles I, being a Member of Parliament was a chancy business. Jermyn had a share of it. He had already been M.P. for Liverpool. In 1640 he was Member for Corfe Castle, and during the Long Parliament for St Edmundsbury. He then made what would appear to have been a mistake. He played a leading part in the first army plot, which was to bring the army down from the north to overawe Parliament, and persisted in it even after lack of backing made it certain that the plot could not be put into operation. As a result he had to flee the country. He did it in style, travelling to Portsmouth in a black satin suit with white boots (hardly a costume to escape notice) and carrying an order from the King that he should be provided with a ship to take him to France.

At the beginning of the Civil War Jermyn was occupied in providing money and troops for the royal cause, but in 1643 he was back in England, acting as secretary to the Queen and colonel of her bodyguard. He commanded the small force which escorted her to Oxford and captured Burton-on-Trent. He was wounded – not seriously; but this must be put against the imputation that he was more prominent in the Court than the field of battle. In the same year he was raised to the peerage, becoming a baron. It was not only the Queen who appreciated him. The King, it is said, found Jermyn's freedom from personal scruples and political principles very useful for his own type of foreign policy, and employed him in a number of delicate missions.

In 1644 he accompanied the Queen to France. He was at that time Governor of Jersey, and as such he tried to sell the Channel Isles to France in exchange for arms; but in this he failed.

It was a striking quality of Jermyn that he never hesitated to attempt anything which might prove profitable, however small the chances of success. He was never ashamed, never discouraged by failure. 'No harm in trying' might well have been his motto. As an example, though knowing nothing whatever about the navy, he intrigued to get himself made Lord High Admiral.

When Henrietta Maria became the Queen Mother Jermyn was a prominent figure at Charles II's court in exile – prominent but not popular. All the traditional royalists were against him. He was even accused of dishonesty. Certainly he had control of the royal finances, and certainly he always kept a carriage and lived in the most comfortable style while the King's chief counsellors had to walk through the streets and live in bed-sitting rooms. But nothing was ever proved against Jermyn. His detractors were no doubt jealous of his influence with the Queen Mother, even with the King himself.

At the Restoration he was well rewarded with an earldom and a number of sinecures. Joint Registrar of the Court of Chancery, Keeper of Greenwich House and Park, High Steward of Kingston, were among the profitable but not arduous posts which he obtained. He was also at different times Lord Chamberlain, Ambassador to France, Plenipotentiary in Paris. He lived very well during his later years. Pepys mentions him several times. St Albans always impressed people by his gambling and good living. But Pepys's most interesting note about him is this piece of gossip recorded on the last night of 1662: 'The Queen-mother is said to keep too great a court now; and her being married to my Lord St Albans is commonly talked of; and that they had a daughter between them in France; how true, God knows.' Almost certainly it was not true. But that it should be common talk is a measure of the intimacy which existed throughout his professional life between Jermyn and Queen Henrietta Maria. Through that intimacy he got all he wanted. He never married, and in a way it is appropriate that the father of clubland should have been a bachelor.

John Evelyn, writing in September 1683, gives a last glimpse of the egocentric who did so much for the future comfort of others. 'Dining with her [the Duchess of Grafton] at my Lord Chamberlain's, met my Lord St Albans, now grown so blind that he could not see to take his meat. He has lived a most easy life, in plenty even abroad, whilst his Majesty was a sufferer; he has lost immense sums at play, which yet, at about eighty year old, he continues, having one that sits by him to name the spots on the cards. He eat and drank with extraordinary appetite. He is a prudent old courtier, and much enriched since his Majesty's return.'

As soon as Pall Mall was opened as a street the name of the Earl of St Albans began to appear with increasing frequency in every document concerning the area. In 1662 the street was 'thought fitt immediately to be repaired, new paved or otherwise amended.' This work was by Act of Parliament put in the charge of paving commissioners, of whom St Albans was one. When the owners of such houses as had faced the ancient highway and therefore backed on the new street petitioned the King for compensation, St Albans was granted through his trustees a lease of most of the ancient highway that he might sub-lease to the tenants, existing and prospective. Thus he would control the sites on the south side of Pall Mall. He had his finger in every plot of land, and worked himself into an excellent position for realising his comprehensive plan. But though he had managed so well with the Queen Mother, King Charles and his ministers were harder to deal with. The whole area was Crown land, and the first leases he was granted ran only until 1691. Less than thirty years, the span of a generation, is too short a time in which to build and enjoy any sort of house, much too short for the magnificent and expensive edifices which St Albans intended. As he complained to the King, 'men will not build Pallaces upon any terms but yet of Inheritance.' He clearly meant to develop the area as quickly as possible and then sell out. He was getting on in years, with no son to take over from him. He had neither the wish nor the capital to remain landlord. But he had to be able to offer long leases, or better still freehold.

On 1 April 1665 St Albans was at last granted the freehold of the site for the *piazza* and of about half of the whole area of St James's Field. Later he obtained a lease of the rest until 1740. Then sales were made and building started. But everything did not work out as the old courtier had planned. His was a grandiose design, essentially French in conception. The French would have carried it through exactly; but the English are not like that. Had the English planned the Champs Elysées for London it would have ended up with a nick in the middle due to some problem of private ownership which nothing could resolve.

Look again at Ogilby and Morgan's map. The area turned out to be more difficult of access than had been intended, the obstructions being of an undignified sort. Those at the two ends of Pall Mall (removed by the time the map was drawn) have already been mentioned. But both ends of Jermyn Street were blocked, while King Street and Charles Street were connected with St James's Street and Haymarket respectively only by narrow pedestrian passages. This must have been due to private rights, probably dating from before the Civil War, as was the little zig-zag in Rider Street where it crosses Bury Street. Similar reasons account for the alleys between King Street and Pall Mall. Crown Passage was given the unstraight shape it still retains because it marked the back of the Physic Garden planted by the herbalist James Parkinson well before 1650.

St Albans achieved for his *faubourg* the domestic and self-sufficient characteristics he had aimed at. But it was never exclusive. Tradesmen, servants, artisans can live without aristocrats, but aristocrats cannot live without them. As for the royal heart of the area, the houses round the square were built uniform, but in a less palatial style than originally intended. Even when granted freehold, people did not want to invest in the most expensive type of house – not there. They preferred the better sites available in Pall Mall, where there was more space, fine gardens, a much pleasanter view.

From the first Pall Mall refused to be a mere side of the frame. Though made viable by the development of the whole area, it was a street in its own right with its own distinct characteristics. Its character derived from the people who lived or worked in the street, or used its buildings for their recreation. It passed through various phases. The details of this development, and the lives of the people concerned, are the theme of the pages which follow.

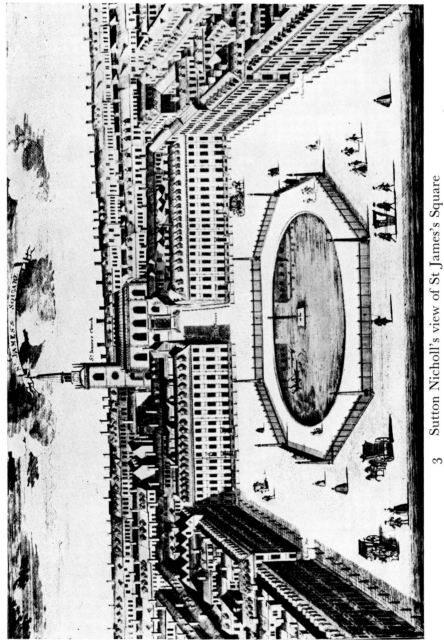

3   Sutton Nicholl's view of St James's Square

4   King Charles talking to Nell Gwyn while Evelyn listens, dis-approvingly. From a painting by Sir Peter Lely

3
Seventeenth-Century Residents

We need not spend much time in picturing the physical appearance of Pall Mall during the first decades of its existence. Houses were sprouting all the while like teeth in a child's mouth. It is better to postpone close inspection until that process is completed.

St Albans began by laying down drains over the whole area. In 1663 the French traveller, Monconys, described Pall Mall as 'au côté d'un grandissime place qui peut être quatre fois la Place Royale'. St James's Square, far from being bigger, is very much smaller than the Place Royale of Paris, so Monconys must have thought that Pall Mall was intended to form the south side of Milord St Albans *piazza* – which in that case would have covered the whole of St James's Field. He could scarcely have made that mistake if there had been any houses on the north side of the street.

The slow start to building was not entirely due to the difficulties over lease and freehold already mentioned. The City tried hard to persuade Parliament to forbid *any* increase in the size of London. Pepys gave what was probably the main reason for this opposition. 'My Lord Mayor told me . . . that this City is as well watered as any city in the world, and that the bringing of water to the City hath cost it, first and last, above £300,000; but by the new building, and the building of St James's by my Lord St Albans, which is now about (and which the City stomach, I perceive, highly, but dare not oppose it), were it now to be done, it would not be done for a million of money.'

Other causes of delay were the plague of 1665 and the Fire of the following year, which would slow up building as does a war. Construction was more rapid during the 1670s, the advantages of Pall Mall as a site having been realized and its reputation as a fashionable address established. But none of these first houses lasted long. Now, only one relic of seventeenth-century Pall Mall remains: This is the centre and right (western) portions of the front of Schomberg House (Nos. 80–81) on the south side of the street just west of the Royal Automobile Club. These two portions of the original façade were retained, and the third (No. 82) reconstructed, when the house – divided into three, with three front doors – was rebuilt in its present form in 1956–58. Schomberg House has a basement completely below ground level, and four storeys above; it is built of vermilion brick with stone dressings. Whether one admires this style or not, it is striking enough to hold its own in any street. There are many incentives to visit it for the sake of its remarkable residents. The first Duke of Schomberg came to England with William of Orange as his second-in-command and was killed at the Battle of the Boyne. His second son, Meinhard, inherited the title from his elder brother, who had not lived long to enjoy it. In 1698 he acquired the house which bears his name and so improved it that within a year its rateable value rose from £4 to £10. Schomberg is mentioned here and there as entertaining in Pall Mall foreign ambassadors and other people of quality. But in 1699 a party of desperately poor disbanded soldiers besieged his house and threatened to pull it down. Though this was prevented, it is interesting that our only relic of the seventeenth century came near to destruction so early in its existence.

Most of the other houses in Pall Mall are the third or fourth to have been built upon the site. In all St James's south of Piccadilly the only seventeenth-century building to remain complete is Wren's parish church.

It is perhaps surprising in a country where the houses of the rich tend to be old and only those of the poor to be new that the buildings of St Albans's aristocratic *faubourg* tumbled down so fast. Many of the first crop were built by speculators, perhaps badly. But as far as Pall Mall is concerned the main reason was more probably that in so elegant a district the purchasers, to most of whom money was little object, sought to express their personalities in their houses. They wanted a new house as a woman would want a new dress. Again and again we read of a purchaser pulling down his purchase and rebuilding, or at least drastically altering.

Whatever the details of style, every house on the south side of Pall Mall was large and fine. They were all, as they still are, on Crown land – with one exception shortly to be mentioned. Since the street ran right up to St James's Palace, the Crown would naturally take a close interest in architecture it would see every day and was entitled to control. We read of some of the houses having forecourts and pleasant gardens at the back. Some of these gardens had raised terraces which made it possible to look over the wall into St James's Park – at the new Mall fringed by elm trees in whose shade the fashionables played or strolled, and beyond it at the lake where one might see King Charles, who liked to mix with his people, exercising his spaniels and feeding his clamorous ducks.

About the new buildings on the north side of Pall Mall it is more difficult to generalize. This was not Crown land. It was granted to St Albans as freehold, and has since passed from one private owner to another. There was therefore much more freedom of architectural choice. There were fewer family houses and more buildings of a commercial nature. Here were the first shops. (Later, some shops appeared on the south side but now all are on the north.) Officers of the Horse Guards took lodgings here. Even when completed the north side was not a continuous line of houses as was the south side before the days of Waterloo Place and Carlton Gardens. It was broken by the two entrances to St James's Square and by narrow passageways – like the present Crown Passage and Royal Opera Arcade – whose residents were then anything but respectable.

This, then, is our picture of seventeenth-century Pall Mall; on the south side of the street spacious houses with gardens; on the north more varied buildings. The difference in elegance between south side and north has always been perceptible.

Who were the seventeenth-century residents of Pall Mall? Many were distinguished and highly respectable, but from the first the street has been full of surprises. There was Sir William Clarke, a man of obscure birth who rose to be Secretary at War during his short residence in Pall Mall. For twelve years he had been secretary to General Monck, first Duke of Albemarle, that enigmatic man who fought for Cromwell and brought back Charles II, and with Monck, after the Restoration, he served on the naval expedition of 1664 against the Dutch. On the second day of the four days' battle he had his right leg shattered by a cannon ball and bore it bravely until he died two days later.

Sir Thomas Clarges was the first to occupy the first house on the site of No. 79. This was built in 1664 or 1665 and was, like all the houses on the south side, on Crown land – though it was to become the only exception to that rule. Clarges as a young man practised medicine, but later worked for General Monck. He carried to Breda Monck's invitation to Charles to return as King. Charles upon reading this knighted Clarges on the spot.

Sir Thomas also owned the adjoining house to the westward of 79. In 1667 he sold these 'two Faire bricke messuages' to Sir William Coventry. Sir William, as General-at-Sea, was largely concerned with the administration of the Navy, and as such was closely associated with Pepys, who visited him at the house and described it as 'very fine'. Pepys thought highly of him. Hyde said that he 'had good parts but was void of religion'. Be that as it may, he left £2,000 for the Protestants expelled from France. He was probably the first resident of Pall Mall to go to prison, being sent to the Tower for challenging the Duke of Buckingham to a duel. Henry Savile in one of his letters said that Coventry had paid £1,400 for the house, which he described as 'one of those pretty handsome ones in Pall Mall by my Lady Ranelagh's'. *//3044.*

Another neighbour was Henry Oldenburg, natural philoso-pher and man of letters, who sometimes signed himself anagram-matically as Grubendal. He was described as being 'of a pechuliar temper which prevented him from agreeing with others'. But he was a friend of Milton, to whom he wrote 'There are two things that I wish to study – Nature and her Creator' – a comprehensive ambition. In 1665 he acted as tutor to Richard Jones, son of Catherine, Lady Ranelagh, who had two houses on the south side of Pall Mall and occupied them both. She was the wife of the second Viscount Ranelagh, and sister of Robert Boyle, the Irish chemist and philosopher, who established Boyle's Law and wrote *The Skeptical Chymist*. He came to live with his sister in Pall Mall, which was more convenient than Oxford for attending meetings of the Royal Society. Here he was often visited by his friend, the physicist Robert Hooke, who also gave his name to a natural Law and who established the principles of the telegraph a hundred years before anyone thought it worth while to apply them. Although history does not so inform us, it may well be that Lady Ranelagh was some-times embarrassed by her chemist brother and his physicist friend. They built on a laboratory where they carried out many experiments. Hooke went further, producing a 'Design' for altering the whole building. Occupying two houses side by side, Lady Ranelagh could hardly say she had no room for her guests.

The family were great house-owners. Richard Jones, the first Earl Ranelagh, owned property all over London – a house in King Street, another in St James's Square, another in Chelsea. It was said that he had 'spent more money, built more fine houses, and laid out more on household furnishing and garden-ing than any other nobleman in England'. He was, says Macky, 'a great epicure and prodigious expensive.' Even in those days it must have been hard to keep up with the Joneses.

One of the most interesting early residents was Sir Samuel

Morland, diplomat, mathematician and inventor. He spent ten years at Magdalene College, Cambridge, where he tutored Pepys; but he took no degree. It is said that as a servant of Cromwell's government he was one day at his desk when Cromwell, Thurloe and Willis, believing themselves alone, discussed a plot to induce Charles and James to land on the Sussex coast on the promise of being met by many royalist supporters, and to murder them. At this stage of the discussion Cromwell noticed Morland, who was pretending to be asleep. The Protector drew his dagger and would have stabbed the eavesdropper if Thurloe had not assured him that Morland had been up working for the last two nights and was certainly sleeping fast. Morland had a knack of getting into trouble. The State Papers record an accusation by Willis that Morland had 'poisoned Cromwell in a posset, and that Thurloe had had a lick of it which had laid him up for a great while.' After the Restoration he went back to science, working on water pumps and corresponding with Pepys on a new type of gun carriage for the navy. He was persuaded not to publish a work *On the Quadrature of Curvilinear Spaces*. He died blind, having invented for himself a type of braille.

Several untitled residents deserve mention. One was John Polixfen, merchant and economic writer, author of *A Discourse on Trade, Coyne and Paper Credit, and of Ways and Means to Gain and Retain Riches*. He was a pre-Socialist in that he preached state control of industry and commerce, but he was fiercely anti-monopolist and gave endless trouble to the East India Company. The second was William de Ryck, a painter of historical subjects, the first artist to be associated with Pall Mall. The third was Joseph Clark, who styled himself 'posture master'. He was quite a fine figure of a man, inclined to stoutness, but his bones were not articulated in the usual way. He could contort his body into extraordinary shapes and alter his face out of recognition. With this strange gift he was also unfortunately possessed of a taste for practical joking. Once, having almost tied his spine into knots, he called as a patient on the celebrated Dr Moleyns. The doctor, presumably after taking his fee, said there was no cure for the disease, whereupon Clark straightened his back. He was the plague of tailors. He used to get himself measured in one posture and go to a fitting in another. A favourite joke on leaving a reception was to transform himself into a crippled beggar at the door. One wonders if he ever tried this on Lady Ranelagh. We cannot help wondering how these neighbours got on together – if they greeted each other when they met, what gossip they listened to or spread about lady residents not yet mentioned. These were of a species which had only just evolved in England – actresses. One was a mistress of Prince Rupert and the other two of King Charles. Only Charles, a lazy man, would have kept two in the same street.

Margaret Hughes was the first woman to take the part of Desdemona. But she was no meek chattel of a warrior. It is stated in the *Memoirs* of Grammont that she 'brought down and greatly subdued his (Prince Rupert's) natural fierceness'. He left all he had to her and their daughter, Ruperta.

Of King Charles' ladies one was Mary Davies, who from 1675 to 1687 owned a house on part of the site of the Army and Navy Club. The other was Nell Gwyn, who first lived in a house on the south side previously occupied by Dr Thomas Sydenham, and moved in 1671 to the house already referred to on the site of the present No. 79, which she took over from Sir William Coventry and which she owned for the rest of her life.

Mary, or Moll Davies, as she was always called, was an actress of the Duke's Theatre, rival of the King's where Nell performed. These two theatres had been reopened at the Restoration after twenty-three years of closure of all such frivolous and ungodly places of amusement. Performances took place at three o'clock, following dinner, at which it was the Restoration custom to drink deep healths unto his Majesty and to make it perfectly clear by conversation and behaviour that one thoroughly disapproved of the excesses of Puritanism. Charles was the first monarch to attend public performances, and – another innovation – women, not boys, took women's parts. The young bloods of the court had learned to take their pleasures where they found them while wandering the continent with their light-hearted master. There was a good deal of sporting with the orange wenches, who were considered fair game. So, though of a slightly higher class, were the actresses. Those of any reputation had distinguished lovers.

Moll Davies won the royal favour after acting Celania in *The Rivals*. She danced a jig in the play and sang a song which began,

My lodging is on the cold ground
And very hard is my fare.

There is a portrait of her by Lely, who must have been kept very busy painting the royal mistresses. She was not beautiful but small, vivacious, bright-eyed, and full of energy. She was a moderately gifted actress who worked hard and was never at fault through any lack of concentration or preparation. Perhaps she attracted a lazy and irresponsible monarch because he would want to make her stop what she felt she ought to be doing and acquiesce in his whim of the moment. From her point of view, since one had to have a lover it was most satisfactory to to have a royal one. It was the best of status symbols, and saved time-wasting over household bills. I doubt whether Moll's heart was touched or that she on her side could touch other hearts. She merely went about with 'By Appointment to His Majesty' invisibly painted on her bustling little carriage.

Nell Gwyn was as different a person as it is possible to imagine. As a strange creation of the Almighty, and as an owner-occupier of Pall Mall for sixteen years, she deserves more documented study. This point must be made at once: she touched the hearts of most of the people who came across her, and she did so without trying. She touched the heart of the King. Whatever virtues Charles II may have had, and there were some, he was throughout his years on the throne essen-

5   Extract from Kip's view of London, 1714–22

6   Early view of Pall Mall

7   View of St James's Palace and Pall Mall
The round cobble-stones referred to by Gay may be distinguished

9   The first Royal Academy

tially self-centred and self-indulgent. When such a man wakes hazily from the stroke he knows will kill him – drowning in a paralysing sea – one would expect his thoughts to be more than ever for himself. But Charles said to his brother and heir, just audibly, 'Let not poor Nelly starve'. Of limited generosity yet human, one likes him for that. And it helps to prove that Nell had that quality, surely the warmest gift of God, of awaking decent sentiments in selfish people. Unblushing sinner though she was, she does not deserve to be dismissed as a harlot, still less to be remembered in a cosy tea-room sort of way. Exactly why her name is so well known in England's long and not inglorious history would make an interesting study in national psychology, but is beyond the scope of this book. It is appropriate, however, to sketch her life as recorded by her contemporaries.

There are several portraits of her by Lely (of course) and others; and she is described as having tiny feet, delicate hands, and a merry laugh which took such charge of her features that her eyes almost disappeared. As the world knows, and as both the Duchess of Portsmouth and Lord Rochester confirm, her first employment in a theatre was as an orange girl, standing with her back to the stage, facing the pit, with a fruit basket covered with vine leaves over her bare arm, calling out, 'Oranges – Will you have any oranges?' This was a job in which a girl had to be able to stand up her for herself, but as will be seen, Nell had a pretty sharp tongue.

She graduated to the stage, where she proved excellent in comedy and very bad in tragedy. She said in one epilogue

I know you in your hearts

Hate serious plays – as I hate serious parts.

Pepys, our first main authority, met her in April 1665, when he was thirty-three and she scarcely fifteen. The occasion was the opening performance at the Duke's Theatre of *Mustapha* by the Earl of Orrery, the enterprising nobleman who imported tea from Holland and sold it at great profit to his friends. *Mustapha* was put on with brand new costumes and scenery. It was an occasion to attract not only the artists from the rival theatre but the King and his court as well – so of course Pepys was there. But he seems scarcely to have noticed the performance. Before going to bed that night he wrote, 'All the pleasure of the play was the King and my Lady Castlemaine were there, and pretty witty Nell . . . which pleased me mightily.' For so young a girl to shine in such company says all that need be said for cockney self-assurance.

Pepys was as constant a theatre-goer as the King. In his frequent references to Nell he was perhaps less objective than usual. He was delighted when she acted a mad part well and cross with her when she had done a serious one badly. He made no secret of his partiality. On the night of 23 January 1667 he wrote, 'Knipp took us all in, and brought us to Nelly, a most pretty woman who acted the great part of Coelia today very fine and did it pretty well: I kissed her and so did my wife; and a mighty pretty soul she is.' A few lines later, summing up the particular pleasures of the day, he concluded, 'and especially the kissing of Nell'. Almost exactly a year later he recorded this piece of gossip, 'That the King did send several times for Nelly, and she was with him; and I am very sorry for it, and can hope for no good to the State from having a Prince so devoted to his pleasure.'

So Nell Gwyn moved up in the world and out of the heart of Pepys; and in due course occupied her first house in Pall Mall. But she continued to act until her first son was on the way. She took her royal lover in her stride. She once remarked in his hearing that he was her Charles III, meaning that she had had two former lovers of that name. The actor Cibber tells a story about a musical party given in her house with Charles and his brother James Duke of York among the audience. The King praised the musicians, whereupon Nell remarked: 'Then, Sir, to show that you do not speak like a courtier, I hope you will make the performers a handsome present.' The King said he had no money on him, and the Duke of York that he had only a guinea or two. Nell turned to the other guests, exclaiming, 'Odds fish ' – Charles's favourite oath – 'What company am I got into?'

It was some time after she had moved to No. 79 (for simplicity I shall use without further explanation the numbers of existing houses) that she discovered that the King had conveyed the lease of the house to her only. That all the buildings on the south side of the street were on Crown land, no private person owning the freehold, meant nothing to her. Dr Heberden says, 'She returned him the lease and conveyances, saying she had always conveyed free under the Crown, and always would; and would not accept it until it was conveyed free to her by an Act of Parliament.' She won her point and ever since No. 79 has been freehold.

Unlike most of her rivals Nell received no title. She seemed to care little about such things. But she was ambitious for her two sons. Though the King was fond of them, and had verbally acknowledged them as his, they were legally plain Charles and James with only their mother's surname. Once when the King was visiting her she called out to one of the boys, 'Come hither, you little bastard'. Charles, shocked for once, protested at her language. 'I have no better name to call him by', said Nell. Very soon her sons were created Charles, Earl of Beaufort (later Duke of St Albans) and James, Lord Beauclerk.

Nell Gwyn's house was one of those with the end of the garden raised to allow a view into the park. The diarist, John Evelyn, less susceptible than Pepys, mentions it in an entry on 1 March 1671: 'I had a fair opportunity of talking to His Majesty about it [some work at Windsor] in the lobby next to the Queen's side, where I presented him with some sheets of my History. I thence walked with him through St James's Park to the garden where I both saw and heard a very familiar discourse between——and Mrs Nelly, as they call an impudent comedian, she looking out of her garden on a terrace at the top of the wall, and——standing on the green walk under it. I was heartily sorry at this scene.' The——s are Evelyn's own.

Nell cared nothing for what the neighbours thought of her. She had her mother to stay with her at No. 79. All we know of this old lady is that she was very fat and fond of brandy. Nell's household bills show that she bought plasters, glysters and cordials for 'old Mrs Gwyn'.

The common people adored her. She was one of themselves, frank, witty, unpretentious. In contrast they hated most of the other royal mistresses as over-expensive luxuries. Louise de Querouaille, Duchess of Portsmouth (whose very foreign name was simplified to Mrs Carwell) was suspect as a Roman Catholic and thoroughly disliked. Once Nell in her coach was mistaken for her and insulted by a mob. Nell put her head out of the window and said cheerfully, 'Pray, good people, be civil; I am the Protestant whore.' Although there is no positive proof of it, there is no reason to doubt the firmly-held tradition that she inspired the hospital for the old soldiers whose successors are called Chelsea Pensioners. She was warm-hearted, generous, careless of money – careless of most things. Although King James II, faithful to his brother's last wish, saved her from starving, she died poor – but not entirely unhappy. In one of her parts she had exclaimed, 'I am resolved to grow fat and look young till forty, and then slip out of the world with the first wrinkle and the reputation of five-and-twenty.' She died at the age of thirty-six.

Nell Gwyn's Pall Mall house was inherited by her surviving son, the Duke of St Albans. (This young man had, of course, no connexion with the Earl of St Albans. The title was purely coincidental – unless Charles had his tongue in his cheek when he conferred it.) The Duke lived there until 1694, when he had to hand over the house to his creditors. The Duke of Schomberg occupied it during 1696–98 while his own house next door was being made ready for him. It then passed to various other owners. In 1766 King George III's younger brother secretly married the Dowager Countess Waldegrave in its drawing-room. It later passed to Dr William Heberden, whose account of the granting of the freehold already has been told. One wonders if his inhabiting the house, and pulling it down, was in any way connected with learning the story. He demolished and rebuilt about 1770. The present No. 79 was built in 1866–68 for the Eagle Insurance Company.

4
New Trends of a New Century

By THE BEGINNING of the eighteenth century the building of Pall Mall's houses had been completed and the street, young though it was, had become one of the best known in London. The return of the Court, with King William III and Queen Mary, to St James's Palace in 1698 had considerably added to its success.

In *Journey through England*, published in 1714, the last year of Queen Anne's reign, John Macky wrote, 'I am lodged in the street called Pall Mall, the ordinary residence of all strangers, because of its vicinity of the Queen's Palace, the Park, the Parliament House, the Theatres, the Chocolate- and Coffee-houses, where the best company frequent. If you would know our manner of living, 'tis thus: we rise by nine, and those that frequent great men's levees find entertainment at these till eleven, or, as in Holland, go to tea-tables; about twelve the beau monde assembles in several coffee- or chocolate-houses; the best of which are the Cocoa-tree and White's Chocolate houses, St James's, the Smyrna, Mrs Rochford's, and the British coffee-houses; and all these so near one another, that in less than an hour you see the company of them all. We are carried to these places in chairs (or sedans), which are here very cheap, a guinea a week, or a shilling per hour, and your chair-men serve you as porters to run on errands, as your gondoliers do at Venice.

'If it be fine weather, we take a turn in the Park till two, when we go to dinner; and if it be dirty, you are entertained at picquet or basset at White's, or you may talk politics at the

Smyrna or St James's. I must not forget to tell you that the parties have their different places, where, however, a stranger is always well received; but a Whig will no more go to the Cocoa-tree than a Tory will be seen at the coffee-house of St James's.

'The Scots go generally to the British, and a mixture of all sorts to the Smyrna. There are other little coffee-houses much frequented in the neighbourhood, – Young Man's for officers; Old Man's for stock-jobbers, pay masters and courtiers; and Little Man's for sharpers. I was never so confounded in my life as when I entered this last; I saw two or three tables full at faro, and was surrounded by a set of sharp faces, that I was afraid would have devoured me with their eyes. I was glad to drop two or three half-crowns at faro to get off with a clear skin, and was overjoyed to be got rid of them.

'At two we generally go to dinner: ordinaries [set meals] are not so common here as abroad, yet the French have set up two or three good ones for the convenience of foreigners in Suffolk Street, where one is tolerably well served; but the general way here is to make up a party at the coffee-house to go to dine at the tavern, where we sit till six, when we go to the play; except you are invited to the table of some great man, which strangers are always courted to and nobly entertained.'

A pleasant life in a pleasant quarter of the town. Look at Kip's view, which was drawn at about this time. Pall Mall has become a stately line of buildings starting with the Palace. One notices the fine gardens behind the south-side houses, the handsome avenues of St James's Park, the deer in the Green Park, the curve of the Thames behind and St Paul's on the horizon. London, although it had already exceeded the limits set by the City, was still by present standards not too large.

Of the chocolate and coffee houses mentioned by Macky several were actually in Pall Mall, not merely in the neighbourhood. The Cocoa Tree was opened in 1698 by Sol De Lafoy on part of the site of the Royal Automobile Club. Under subsequent owners it remained there, being mentioned in *The Spectator,* and by Swift who described himself as an *habitué,* until 1757 when it moved across the street to the site of the Army and Navy. Early in its career it became a Tory stronghold, so much so that it was claimed that Prince Charles Edward's coach would stop there of its own accord if Brigadier Mordaunt drove it to London after Culloden. In the reign of George III it became a club, and its story will be resumed when we reach that stage of this history.

The Whig stronghold, St James's, was not unnaturally in St James's Street. So was White's. In passing one may mention that this street, which might well have rivalled Pall Mall as a place of residence, and in fact was meant to, developed rather as a place of fashionable trade. Its clubs unquestionably rivalled those of Pall Mall later on, but in the early eighteenth century its houses were less distinguished.

That its customers were 'a mixture of all sorts' was the general reputation of the Smyrna, a small three-storeyed house which stood on the north side of Pall Mall, to the east of Crown Passage. It was opened in 1702 and remained on that site for seventy years. Swift, Prior and Steele frequented it, the last named writing in *The Tatler* about the 'cluster of wise-heads, as they are found sitting every evening, from the left side of the fire at the Smyrna, to the door'.

Another famous Pall Mall chocolate house, and a haunt of Tories in the early eighteenth century, was Ozinda's. It had a most favourable position in front of St James's Palace, but was demolished in 1748 when the street thereabouts was widened. William Byrd of Virginia in his *London Diary* (1717–1721) says that the main attractions of the place were drinking chocolate, betting, and reading the newspapers. The same might have been said of any of the chocolate and coffee houses, except for a choice of beverages – with tea as time went on overtaking the other two in popularity – and with political discussion inevitably following the newspaper reading. The Englishman abroad has the reputation of being strong and silent – at least the latter. Nor does he – compared, for instance, with the Latins – shine in conversation with women. But, when comfortable and moderately stimulated, on his own ground and among his own sex, he is strong and talkative. Charles II, whose reign saw the rise of coffee houses and whose conscience as monarch was perhaps not quite at ease, disliked these establishments for the free speech which went on there among all manner of men. He issued a Proclamation to suppress them as nurseries of idleness and pragmaticalness. But he lacked courage to make it effective. So these unofficial parliaments continued to prosper well into the eighteenth century and until many of them formed into clubs – clear thoughts in an atmosphere of tobacco smoke. *The Tatler* recommended its readers before entering a coffee house to prepare their bodies with a dish of tea and to purge their brains with two pinches of snuff.

Pall Mall was adequately supplied with taverns, if not so abundantly as the rest of London. At one time and another there were no less than three all called 'The Star and Garter', which is confusing for the historian. Two of them achieved some fame. One, which flourished in the first half of the eighteenth century, was at No. 44 on the north side, opposite Schomberg House, and is now the office of the Royal Exchange Assurance. The most famous was on the south side where the Carlton Club was until it was bombed and where the so-called No. 100 Pall Mall now stands. Apart from use by private individuals the better taverns – as opposed to the gin houses of the poor – were used for the meetings of societies, much as the Rotary meet in public premises. Swift wrote to Stella: 'I made our Society change their House, and we met today at the Star and Garter in Pall Mall.' The Society of Dilettanti met there when James Fynmore was the licensee, and tried unsuccessfully to buy the premises.

Here, too, took place the duel – if so it may be called – between Lord Byron, great-uncle of the poet, and Mr Chaworth, his neighbour in Nottinghamshire. The two had dined with a company of other gentlemen on the second floor of the tavern, and had got into an argument as to which had the more game on his estate. Mr Chaworth rose. 'Your lordship knows where to find me, in Berkeley Row', he said. He paid his bill and went out. Lord Byron followed and hailed him while he was still on the stairs. The two men went down together to the first floor landing and called to a waiter to show them an empty room. The waiter did so, placed the tallow candle he was carrying on the table, and went out. A few minutes later the bell rang (it was never established who pulled the cord) and the waiter returned. In the gloom of the ill-lighted room he saw the two men standing close together with drawn swords in their hands. He ran and fetched his master. When Fynmore arrived with half a dozen of the guests they found Byron standing with his left arm round Chaworth and his sword in his right. Chaworth held his sword in his left, his right arm being over Byron's shoulder and round his neck. Both men gave up their swords, and a surgeon was sent for.

But though Chaworth was mortally wounded, he had the strength to give this account of the affair. When they had been left in the room by the waiter, Byron had asked him if his last remark about game had been addressed to him or to Sir Charles Sedley, one of the company at dinner. Chaworth had answered, 'If you have anything to say we had better shut the door', and while he was doing this Byron had called on him to draw. As he turned from the door Chaworth saw that Byron's sword was half out of the scabbard. He whipped out his own, made the first thrust, and touched. In the dim light he could not see that he had only pierced the other's waistcoat. He asked whether Byron was mortally wounded. While he was speaking, Byron shortened his sword and stabbed him in the belly. Such was Chaworth's account. He forgave Byron and hoped that the world would too. Byron was tried by his peers in the House of Lords and found guilty of manslaughter. But he claimed benefit of a statute of Edward VI and was discharged.

This unsavoury affair was fortunately by no means the last thing remembered about the Star and Garter. In the middle of the century the Jockey Club – 'our jovial club' as Gilly Williams called it – used to meet there. And in 1774 a committee of peers and gentlemen, convened there to revise the laws of cricket, introduced the leg-before-wicket penalty.

St James's, aristocratic as it was, had its poor. The Haymarket and St James's Market were invaded after closing time by 'finders' who lived on whatever rubbish had been left behind. The narrow passageways between King Street and Pall Mall were said to be the haunts of 'desperate characters', which in history often means much the same as poor. There were robberies. Not so many as today, perhaps, but enough to make a pamphlet writer of 1731 complain of coaches being held up in Pall Mall and of the 'multitude of lewd and disorderly persons [who] throng the streets as soon as evening may be said to begin.'

Gay's *Beggars' Opera* is not all comedy: it gives a grim enough picture of the London of his time. His *Trivia* of 1716 is a lesser work, in indifferent verse, but worth paraphrasing here. We are wakened by street cries which begin early and go on all day. We look out of the window at a threatening sky, and so go out in our second-best wig. Outside, the many signs of taverns and shops are creaking and rumbling in the rising wind. Down comes the rain. Women cover their heads with their riding hoods or slop through the mud in pattens. A team of asses is driven by to the house of someone who has been ordered by the physician to drink their milk. The carts and waggons, which have no springs, rumble noisily over the round stones of the street. The pavements are crowded with people of all sorts – tradesmen, maidens, cripples, beggars, bullies, shoe blacks, chimney sweeps and the occasional fop 'whose mantling peruke veils his empty head' – all trying to avoid being pushed off the pavement into the gutter, which runs with every sort of filth.

The stench is dreadful.

But there is one haven:
Oh, bear me to the paths of fair Pell-mell!
Safe are thy pavements, grateful is thy smell;
At distance rolls along the gilded coach
Nor sturdy carmen on thy walks encroach:
No louts would bar thy ways, were chairs denied,
The soft supports of laziness and pride;
Shops breathe perfumes, thro' sashes ribbons glow,
The mutual arms of ladies, and the beau.
Yet still even here when rains the passage hide
Oft the loose stone spurts up the muddy tide
Beneath thy careless foot; and from on high,
Where masons mount the ladder, fragments fly;
Mortar and crumbled lime in showers descend
And o'er thy head destructive tiles impend.

There was always this danger, for some building was sure to be coming down or going up. It would be difficult almost to the point of impossibility to chart every instance of this continuous change: furthermore it would be dull; sufficient to give an indication of the evolution of Pall Mall.

Between 1719 and 1761 there were a couple of houses on the site of No. 104, one of them occupied by the Earl of Egmont. In the latter year these were taken down and a larger, Palladian-fronted house built in their place. This later became the property of Lady Louisa Manners, then of the Countess of Dysart, until in 1836 it was occupied by the Reform Club, which eventually added this site to that of the present building. This is an example of buildings on the south side coalescing to form fewer and larger ones. Four other buildings also went into the site of the Reform.

Buckingham House, No. 91, is another example of the growth of a building, and of the owner's name as well. From 1710 to 1726 it was occupied by Thomas Pitt, father of the Earl of Londonderry and grandfather of the Earl of Chatham. In 1737

37

it was bought by Richard Grenville. He inherited the title of Earl Temple, called himself George Nugent Temple Grenville, bought the adjoining house and added it to his old one. When he became Marquis of Buckingham he called it Buckingham House, employing the architect Soane for the extensive alterations. Buckingham House was still further improved by the first Marquis's son, Richard Temple Nugent Brydges Chandos Grenville, first Duke of Buckingham and Chandos. There we may leave it, pending the era of clubs, when – having been a section of the War Office – it became part of the R.A.C.

On the north side there was not the same tendency for the houses to coalesce. They remained comparatively small and individual. In 1740 Daniel Graham, His Majesty's Apothecary, pulled down the three houses he owned – 9, 11, 12 – and built three more. His family occupied one of them until the end of the century, when it passed to William Cobbett, the economist and politician, who lived there on his return from America.

One more house on the north side deserves mention because there started in it two interesting trends. It was the house, built in 1726, later numbered 52. It stood between Angel Court and Pall Mall Place (then called King's Place), and was about opposite the house where Nell Gwyn had lived. In 1738 Robert Dodsley set up as a bookseller in No. 52. A bookseller's is one of the comparatively small class of shops where people always make their own purchases, never if they can help it through a proxy, and where moreover they tend to linger and discuss. Dr Johnson developed the habit of doing this at Dodsley's. It was a bookseller, Tom Davis, who introduced Boswell to Johnson, and it was Dodsley of Pall Mall who made an important suggestion to Johnson.

Boswell, writing of the year 1747 when the intended publication of the *Dictionary of the English Language* was first announced in a *Prospectus*, says: 'How long this immense undertaking had been the object of his contemplation, I do not know ... I have been informed by Mr James Dodsley that several years before this period, when Johnson was one day sitting in his brother Robert's shop, he heard his brother suggest to him that a dictionary of the English Language would be a work that would be well received by the publick; that Johnson seemed at first to catch at the proposition, but, after a pause, said in his abrupt and decisive manner, "I believe that I shall not undertake it".'

Thirty-two years later, in 1779, this scrap of conversation is recorded: 'He [Johnson] said, "Dodsley first mentioned to me the scheme of an English Dictionary; but I had long thought of it." Boswell: "You did not know what you were undertaking." Johnson: "Yes, sir, I knew very well what I was undertaking – and very well how to do it – and have done it very well." '

The first trend in Pall Mall was towards leisurely, personal, selective shopping and the consequent discursive encounter of men of similar interests and culture – turning a shop into a kind of club, in fact, before the birth of clubs. The second was towards a wider interest in art. Before the middle of the eighteenth century London had no exhibitions or galleries. Unless one could afford to travel abroad or had access to private collections one never saw good pictures. Reproductions were almost as difficult to get a sight of unless included in books, which were expensive.

The Dodsley bookshop continued until 1788. It was acquired by Alderman John Boydell (later Lord Mayor), who pulled it down and commissioned the architect, George Dance, to build the Shakespeare Gallery, a small yet imposing stone-fronted building in something of a classic style. Boydell, an engraver by profession, must have been a man of considerable fortune and of clear vocation. He commissioned half a dozen or more of the best painters of the day to paint pictures of scenes from Shakespeare, and prints were made from these. How lavish was his expenditure on this project is shown by a letter of Sir Joshua Reynolds, which recorded that Boydell had left £500 on his table as 'earnest money' with a promise of as much more as he should demand.

The Shakespeare Gallery was at first most successful. Its popularity with the literary and artistic proved the need for such an exhibition building. Other and similar private ventures were started. But there were many severe critics who accused Boydell of being purely commercial in his aims. In other words the Shakespeare Gallery was not only a fashionable meeting-place but a lively subject for discussion. It continued until the end of the century, when Boydell, who had expended more than £100,000 on it, was hard hit by the French wars, which closed the continent as a market for his prints. He showed imagination in his method of disposing of the Gallery. He raffled it, selling 22,000 tickets. It was later leased by the British Institution for Promoting the Fine Arts.

5
Art in Pall Mall

IN PROPER HANDS the pen is mightier than the sword, but the wielders of the paint-brush are often the fiercest antagonists. John Boydell was not a painter, and in his treatment of artists he was open-minded as well as open-handed. Besides, the Shakespeare Gallery was his private venture. Therefore, if its life was comparatively short it was harmonious. But the artists fought for twenty years before founding their own, and the nation's, Academy – this at a time when England possessed the best artists she had ever had or perhaps has had until today. Pall Mall was concerned in every phase of this stormily born but finally successful development.

The Society of Dilettanti consisted of young and wealthy amateurs of art; not artists themselves, but the type of men who stocked the stately homes of England with pictures and statuary from Italy. They held a meeting at the King's Arms in Pall Mall in 1749, at which they discussed the formation of an academy of artists for instructional purposes; but nothing came of this. Six years later a group of artists suggested to the Dilettanti that they should together form an academy for both instruction and exhibition. But the Dilettanti, whose financial support was all that the artists wanted, insisted that they should elect the president and have the controlling voice. This was a condition which professional artists could not accept, and the project came to nothing.

The position then became more complicated, with a Society of Arts, a Society of Artists, and a Free Society of Artists all jostling for position. Exhibitions by one or another of these were held in the Strand, in Spring Gardens, and at the rooms of the auctioneers, Lambe and Christie, which were in Pall Mall. These exhibitions, though fairly successful financially (except for those of the Free Society), led to many disputes by the exhibitors about the hanging of their pictures, for since they all wanted the best positions it was impossible to please everyone.

In 1765 the Society of Artists became by Royal Charter the Incorporated Society of Artists of Great Britain. This gave it the ascendancy. But very soon it was split in two by quarrels. The factions were led by William Chambers (later knighted) and James Paine. The latter gained control, but Chambers then played his trump card. He had been tutor in architecture to George III when that king was Prince of Wales, and going to him, he proposed the setting up of an Academy under royal patronage. He evidently knew how to handle his ex-pupil, for on 1 December 1768 King George signed the Instrument for the foundation of the Royal Academy, which was to be both a school for students and a place of exhibition for the works of artists of 'distinguished merit, where they may offer their performances to public inspection, and acquire that degree of reputation and encouragement which they shall be deemed to deserve.' The forty Academicians were to take turns in supervising the students during the winter and summer, and the King accepted financial responsibility until the Academy should be able to stand on its own feet. Although this was soon achieved, the custom of submitting the business of the Academy to the Sovereign in person has always been maintained.

The Royal Academy's premises were in Pall Mall, in the house of Richard Dalton, a minor artist who himself had tried to form an academy. The house stood on part of the site of the present United Service Club, opposite to Market Lane, so called because it led from Pall Mall to St James's Market (it is now named Royal Opera Arcade). The school and library were moved to Somerset House in 1771, but the Academy held its annual exhibitions in Pall Mall until 1779. Here, too, were held the annual dinners to which the Academy has always invited both distinguished patrons of art and leaders of other professions. The high standard of speeches which characterizes these dinners was set by the Academy's first President, Joshua Reynolds, who held this office from 1768 to 1792.

Sir Joshua Reynolds, Thomas Gainsborough, George Romney; these three great men were born in that order and within a dozen years. From the first there was discussion as to which was the greatest artist. But only Reynolds had the qualities necessary for a President of the Academy. This was because he was by no means only a painter; he was a shrewd, cultured, sociable man of the world. He kept out of the early quarrels associated with the birth of the Academy. (So, for that matter, did Gainsborough and Romney – because they were not interested.) At the time of the split in the Incorporated Society of Artists Reynolds went with Burke on a visit to Paris. He was cautious enough also to make no friendships with fellow artists so close as to be embarrassing; but he was the very opposite of unsociable. He held frequent informal dinners at his house in Leicester Square, and was an intimate friend of Johnson, Burke, Goldsmith, Gibbon, and Garrick. Here is the key to the most interesting facet of the character of the Academy's first President. His position made his the predominant voice in questions of art. In the opinion of many he was the greatest painter of his day: some thought him the greatest in the world. But his secret ambition was literary. He wanted to be remembered as a writer. He was the founder of the Literary Club. This is far from the only instance in history of the master of one art losing his heart to another. But fortunately in the case of Reynolds the infatuation was in no way ridiculous, for he knew what to do with words.

Dr Johnson, who said more than anyone except Shakespeare, once remarked, 'A man is most successfully flattered by being supposed to possess virtues to which he has the least pretentions.' Reynolds was flattered in this way. In the dedication to him of *The Deserted Village* Goldsmith wrote, 'You can gain nothing from my admiration, as I am ignorant of that art in which you are said to excel, and I may lose much by the severity of your judgement, as few have a juster taste in poetry than you.' And Boswell, dedicating his *Life of Johnson,* said to Reynolds, 'Your excellence, not only in the Art over which you have long presided with unrivalled fame, but also in Philosophy and elegant Literature, is well known to the present, and will continue to be the admiration of future eyes.'

This is high praise from writers of poetry and prose who kept always in mind their reputations in the arts in which they had pretensions. Dr Johnson's remark, if he had Reynolds in mind, was inappropriate in that Reynolds had considerable pretensions as a writer. He took endless trouble over the preparation of his *Discourses,* which were read at meetings of the Academy. But for Reynolds 'writer' is more appropriate than 'orator', for he spoke badly, having damaged his lip in a fall from a horse. Moreover, he was deaf, which made it harder for him to correct his enunciation.

Some critic-biographers in search of original material who peer through dusty keyholes into private rooms of the past have suggested that Reynolds had not got it in him to write as he did, and that therefore Johnson and Burke must have been his ghosts. Certainly he gained from conversation with them and other literary friends. Probably he was influenced by their style. Occasionally they may have suggested the way to convey a thought. But the thoughts of the *Discourses* are those of a painter. Such manuscripts as remain show only a word or a phrase altered here and there by another hand.

'Besides furnishing able men to direct the student', Reynolds said at the Inauguration, 'this Academy is a repository for the great examples of Art.' (There was no other in London before the birth of the National Gallery, and the Academy very soon acquired among other masterpieces the Cartoon of the Virgin and St Anne by Leonardo da Vinci which has lately been in the news.) 'Every seminary of learning', he went on, 'may be said to be surrounded with an atmosphere of floating knowledge, where every mind may imbibe somewhat congenial to its own original conceptions. Knowledge thus obtained has always something more popular and useful than that which is forced upon the mind by private conceptions or solitary meditation.'

His advice did not, as this passage taken alone might suggest, advocate merely waiting for inspiration. He discountenanced 'that false and vulgar opinion that rules are the fetters of genius'. He encouraged a deep study of first principles. In another *Discourse,* speaking of the examples of the Old Masters hanging on the walls, he said, 'Study them with a suspicion that great men are not always exempt from great faults: but remember that it is their excellencies which have taught you their defects.' This is not only good artistic advice but good prose. What matters here about Reynolds's literary and philosophical side is that he attracted to the new Academy in Pall Mall not only painters and those interested in that art, but also literary men. He was a tireless worker, painting until the light made it impossible. But in the evenings he enjoyed the company of his various men friends or went to a *conversazione* of the bluestockings, Mrs Montagu, Mrs Vesey or Miss Monkton. These, and those in their wide circle of acquaintances, male and female, came to see the permanent pictures and, of course, the annual exhibitions, which were very fully covered by the Press at that time. Many of the exhibits were portraits. Sometimes there were portraits of the same well-known person by two, or even three, artists. This was good copy for the journalists of the day. One way and another, Reynolds and the Academy added a very great deal to the cultural life of Pall Mall.

Another painter deserves quite as much attention, for he painted as well as exhibited in Pall Mall. At midsummer 1774 Thomas Gainsborough came up to London from Bath, where he had already made a brilliant reputation, and took the western portion of Schomberg House at a rent of £150 a year, later reduced for some reason to £132. There he lived and worked for the rest of his life, as a blue plaque over the door records.

Gainsborough would not have made a good President of the Academy. He took not the slightest interest in its proceedings, looking on it merely as a place to hang his pictures. When they were, in his opinion, hung badly he wrote to the Council:

Mr Gainsborough presents his compliments to the Gentlemen appointed to hang the pictures at the Royal Academy; and begs leave to *hint* that if the Royal Family, which he has sent to this Exhibition (*being less than three quarters*) are hung upon the line with full-lengths, he never more, whilst he breathes, will send another picture to the Exhibition. This he swears by God.

The pictures referred to were fifteen heads and busts of the Royal Family, a measure of the success he had so quickly attained in London. He wrote again on a much friendlier note to the Secretary personally, explaining how the hanging should be done, and enclosing a sketch. He was impulsive, not at all diplomatic. But he interests us, for one thing, because of the procession of beautiful women whom he brought to this stronghold of masculinity to pose for their portraits in his studio.

One of the loveliest of these was the Honourable Mrs Graham, whose full-length portrait now hangs in the National Gallery of Scotland. Its story is told in William Whitley's biography of Gainsborough. Mrs Graham was married at seventeen, on the same day as her sister, and spent part of her honeymoon in London where the portrait was painted. She was, it was said, a lady not only of exceptional beauty and elegance, as her picture shows, but also of great charm. Her husband, Graham of Balgowan, later Lord Lynedoch, was a man of courage. While in London he was escorting his young wife and her sister to a party in Grosvenor Square. On the way their coach was stopped by highwaymen, who were still active even in the middle of London. Two men seized the horses'

46

heads while a third opened the carriage door and at pistol point demanded money and jewels. Graham, who was sitting on the far side of the coach, leapt across the two ladies, grappled with the thief, and carried him to the ground before he could fire, falling on top of him. This one was handed over to the watch; the other two ran away. Graham and the ladies went on to Grosvenor Square, where Graham had to keep behind his wife so that her ample skirt would hide his muddy trousers.

For seventeen years they were ideally happy. Then Mrs Graham's health began to fail. Her husband took her from Balgowan to the hot-wells of Bristol, then to the south of France. But off Hyères she died at sea. He determined to take her body home – by canal to Toulouse and then down the Garonne to Bordeaux. The year was 1792; France was in the throes of revolution. At Toulouse he was stopped by a drunken mob of municipal guards and volunteers who tore the coffin open to make sure it contained no contraband. In these circumstances the husband, already almost frantic with grief, saw his dead wife again.

Back in Scotland he could find no peace. Nor could he bear to look at the portrait. He sent it away, none knew where, and volunteered for the army. He was then forty-four, an advanced age at which to become a soldier. But he fought the French with such courage and skill that he won a peerage and the rank of general. He died, a distinguished old soldier, sixty-nine years after his marriage. Then his heir received a letter from the keeper of a warehouse in London – and the portrait reappeared.

An equally romantic story concerns another of Gainsborough's sitters, Mary Robinson, a young actress of quite remarkable beauty who became an intimate friend of the Prince of Wales after appearing as Perdita in *A Winter's Tale,* being known thereafter as 'Perdita'. But the Prince, in the opinion of most people, treated her badly and threw her over. This won her much sympathy and popularity, as her beauty won her many admirers. But her deep and only true love was a dashing and not particularly reputable cavalry officer, Colonel Tarleton.

At the height of her fame and fortune – though only in her early twenties – Perdita was rich enough to commission portraits of herself by Gainsborough, Romney, and Reynolds, all three.

One winter's day she heard from Tarleton that he must have £800 immediately. (It sounds like a debt of honour.) Unless it was forthcoming at once he would have to flee the country. She offered to go with him, but he refused. He then left her, promising to meet her again that night at the opera. Perdita could not lay her hands on so large a sum at short notice, but she did raise £300, with a promise of the rest in the morning, and with this she went to meet Tarleton. But he had vanished. Guessing correctly that he had decided to run for it, and knowing the port from which he intended to sail, she took a post-chaise in pursuit at three o'clock in the morning. She was hot and agitated, dressed for the opera, not the road, and it was a bitterly cold night. She fell into a numbed sleep. At the first stage she was carried into the inn half dead with cold. She never walked again. From the age of twenty-four she was a cripple who had to be carried from one room to another. It was a long time before she even recovered the use of her fingers, but when she did this courageous woman made a living by her pen, contributing for some time to the *Morning Post*. Nor did she give up her social life. Reynolds was often a guest at her parties. But she was not the sort of person who can live sensibly on a small income. Financial crises came, and recurred. She had to sell her possessions one after another. Thus she lost the portraits of herself before she was crippled.

The sale of her Gainsborough is a cynical incident. In 1785 her furniture and effects were seized and put up for auction. The Gainsborough portrait was displayed between prints of Tarleton and the Prince of Wales. The auctioneer opened by saying that if a security for £250 were offered the sale would not proceed. But none was forthcoming, and when the auction

Gainsborough

Christie

Reynolds

The 'wicked' Lord Lyttleton

10 'Perdita' Robinson from the portrait by Gainsborough

started there were few bidders. The Gainsborough was knocked down for thirty-two guineas, and is said to have been bought by someone acting for the Prince of Wales. There are grounds for believing this, for it was in the possession of the Prince in 1790. From him it passed to the Marquis of Hertford, and it is now in the Wallace Collection in Hertford House.

Many women of title as well as beauty went to the studio at Schomberg House. Gainsborough worked at lightning speed, bringing canvases to life. What is it which enables such an artist not merely to create a likeness but to capture a particular trait? Surely it is the art of conversation which makes the subject unguarded and betrays the hidden part. This is a two-edged sword. The painter paints what he sees, good or bad. This was the comment of the *Morning Chronicle* on Gains-borough's portrait of Lord Chesterfield which was shown at the Academy in 1778: 'The painter has so happily caught his Lordship's character that the countenance of the portrait has in it all the insensibility and want of meaning for which the original is remarkable.'

Gainsborough was witty, lively, unconventional. Not only did lovely women and distinguished men visit his studio: pigs and donkeys also went through the front door and up the stairs of Schomberg House. His country scenes had to have their models. He is still more famous for his landscapes than for his portraits. And his private ambition was music, in which he was more than competent. On many evenings at his house music was played and good wine drunk.

A hidden trait of Gainsborough's was incidentally brought out in an article published in the *St James's Chronicle* shortly after the death of his friend, the German musician Abel. With reference to the latter we read:

Justly admired as he was for his public performances, it was only a few of his intimate friends in private who were witnesses of his wonderful musical powers, to come at which, however, a bottle or two of good Burgundy before him and his viol da gamba within his reach were necessary. In that situation friends would introduce the subject of the human passions, and Abel, not very capable of expressing in English his own sentiments, would catch up his viol da gamba and tell the story of Lefèvre thereon until he brought tears to the eyes of his hearers; and not lay it down till he had made his friend Gainsborough dance a hornpipe on the bottom of a pewter quart pot.

The artist, evidently, was easily moved to jollity as well as sorrow. Another nice story of him illustrates a hyper-suggestive trait. While dining with Garrick, Gainsborough met Dr Johnson who ever after in conversations with Garrick referred to Gainsborough as 'your sprightly friend' or gave him the adjective 'ingenious'. The other side of the story is that Gainsborough was intrigued by the Doctor's mannerisms and involuntary movements – so much so that having imitated them at first for fun he found it difficult to break the habit and for a month or two continued to twitch and gesticulate.

Gainsborough quarrelled with Reynolds. They were close rivals, though Reynolds always praised his work. But Reynolds went to Schomberg House when Gainsborough lay dying, and they were reconciled. Gainsborough's last words to him were the famous: 'We are all going to heaven, and Van Dyck is of the company.' If he was right, heaven must have some good pictures by now.

6
The Varied Experiences of an Auctioneer

THE ROYAL ACADEMY, the President with his wide circle of literary and social friends, Gainsborough with his studio, his musical friends and more bohemian habits – it is easy to understand how much Pall Mall was visited and talked about before the end of the century which followed its inception. But there was another man of another profession who lived and worked in the Street and added very considerably to its reputation. This was James Christie. To set him in focus at the start: when Gainsborough's portrait of Christie was exhibited it was said by the art critic of the *Morning Chronicle* to be so good a likeness that printing the name of the subject was superfluous. How many auctioneers would one now recognize at once from their pictures?

James Christie is said to have been born in Perth, in 1730, his father being an Englishman of good family and his mother Scottish, a close relation of Prince Charlie's Flora Macdonald. Even this scant information is doubtful, but one likes to believe he had the blood of Flora Macdonald in his veins. More than erudition and business sense was needed for a young auctioneer to become a popular and respected figure in the exclusive society of his time, and to found a firm which has been internationally famous for nearly two hundred years. That extra something was the hypnotizing charm more often found among mystical Celts than down-to-earth Anglo-Saxons. Gainsborough's portrait of him suggests a man hard to resist.

There are plenty of contemporary accounts of his appearance and character. He was tall and dignified, remarkable for eloquence and professional enthusiasm, and was an intimate friend of Garrick, Reynolds, Gainsborough and other men of note. John Taylor in his *Records of My Life* says, 'There was something interesting and persuasive as well as thoroughly agreeable in his manner. He was very animated and, it may be justly said, eloquent in his recommendations of any article to be announced from his "Rostrum"; as well as in occasional effusions of genuine humour. He was courteous, friendly and hospitable in private life and was held in great esteem by his numerous friends, among whom there were many of high rank.' Incidentally, the rostrum referred to continued to be used until Christie's was hit by a bomb and burned out in 1940.

Christie was at first a midshipman. That he had the reputation of a man of action is proved by one of the stories about him. When the house of Admiral Sir Hugh Pallister (it stood on the site of the Junior Carlton) was attacked by a mob, Christie, a near neighbour, led out his male servants armed with sticks and drove off the trouble-makers in confusion. This story suggests that Christie became a legend in his lifetime – and shows that one can't trust a legend. The truth is that the mob gutted Pallister's house and burnt his effigy in the street, presumably using his furniture as fuel. Hugh Pallister, after some thirty years of active and honourable service, had been created a baronet and a Lord of the Admiralty with the rank of Rear-Admiral. Three events in his earlier career are worth mentioning. As a Lieutenant in 1743 he brought a charge of cowardice against his commander, Sir John Norris. It took moral courage for a junior officer to do such a thing, and he seems to have been justified, for Norris fled the country before court-martial. Also while a junior officer Pallister suffered a painful wound from an accidental explosion and was on the sick list for a considerable time: if his health was not permanently affected, control of his temper certainly was. During one of his early commands he took a convoy from England to America by the then almost unused southern route, and arrived with healthy and cheerful crews in less than eight weeks. He was not lacking in initiative and skill.

While still holding his appointment at the Admiralty Pallister was in 1778 posted for active service under Admiral Keppel. They were engaged for three days in an intermittent action with the French. During the fighting Pallister's ship fell to leeward. The French drawing off, Keppel made the signal to re-form. Instead of obeying, Pallister attempted to engage the French ships as they ran for harbour, until it was evident that he could achieve nothing alone. Only then did he rejoin the line. Why he disobeyed orders – unfortunately for him without success – is most plausibly explained by bad temper aroused by the order to re-form. Keppel took no action against Pallister, but immediately sailed with him on another cruise.

While they were away the newspapers launched a campaign against Pallister on the ground that the failure of the action was due to him. Returning to England, Pallister asked Keppel to deny the charges. Keppel refused, and at Pallister's demand Keppel was court-martialled, but was acquitted. It was then that the mob worked off their fury on Pallister's house. Pallister resigned as a Lord of the Admiralty and submitted himself for court-martial. Keppel refused to make a charge. With no prosecutor and no charge the trial was more in the nature of a court of enquiry, but it lasted for twenty-one days before a packed house. Pallister was acquitted of misconduct, but neither unanimously nor with honour. The only appointment he obtained thereafter was the Governorship of Greenwich Hospital. He died a bachelor and left most of his fortune to his son.

His neighbour and ally, John Christie, who had started work as an auctioneer in partnership elsewhere in London, set up on his own in Pall Mall in 1766. He first used rooms in the house of

Richard Dalton, opposite the Royal Opera Arcade, where the Academy began. In 1768 he acquired the lease of Lady Ranelagh's two houses (or those which replaced them), Nos. 83 and 84, and moved into No. 83, sub-letting the other. He thus became a next-door neighbour of Gainsborough, and worked on part of the site of the Royal Automobile Club. Habitués of the R.A.C. bar should therefore cast their imaginations back first to chocolate drinking (this being the original site of the Cocoa Tree), and also to high art and auctioneering.

Christie spent £1,000 on building his Great Auction Room in the garden, approached by a passage between his two houses. This was the firm's place of business until it moved to King Street in 1823.

At first Christie was by no means exclusively concerned with works of art. He sold land and houses, animals, '72 loads of excellent meadow hay', anything that came to hand. In his second catalogue is listed the household furniture of a gentleman going abroad, 'to which is added the rich wearing apparel, fine laces, jewels, etc. of his Intended Lady, deceased, preparatory for his nuptials.'

When Christie began to sell pictures even his persuasive notes in the catalogue and his eloquence at the rostrum could not push prices above a level which now seems ridiculously low. This was not because money was worth much more then than now, but because the monetary value of pictures was much less. A gentleman would bid higher for a horse than for an Old Master. Tattersall, a contemporary auctioneer, encountered less sales resistance. At Christie's first picture sale a Titian went for two guineas. Nor were works of recent or contemporary interest considered of much more value. In 1768 Christie offered a work by Sir Peter Lely which he described in the Catalogue as 'a capital picture of King Charles II, in the character of Cymon, looking at the Duchesses of Cleveland and Portland and Nell Gwyn asleep, with the most graceful parts of their bodies exposed.' It was knocked down for £8. 7s. 6d.

54

The most remarkable instance of pictures going for low prices was the sale of Sir Joshua Reynolds' private collection. There were four hundred and eleven works in all, among which were said to be included fifty-four by Correggio, seventy by Van Dyck, thirty-two by Tintoretto, twelve by Leonardo da Vinci, forty-four by Michelangelo, twenty-two by Rubens, twenty-four by Raphael, nineteen by Rembrandt. Imagine what would have been bid for those pictures now! The whole lot went in 1794 for a total of £10,319. Many must have been copies, or this total makes no sense at all. Even so they would be good copies, and they had been the personal choice of the first President of the Royal Academy, as popular as a man as he was famous as an artist – and only dead two years. That was a bad day, for Christie had by then begun to get quite good figures. His sales were lively affairs, particularly when his friends Garrick and Gainsborough were present, as they often were. The witty exchanges of this couple put everyone in a good humour. Christie said that their presence added fifteen per cent to the receipts.

Perhaps he was not so good at the melancholy business of acting as a sort of undertaker to the possessions of friends. He sold Gainsborough's pictures after his death. The total sum received is not known, but *The Mall* is said to have gone for £115. 10s. 0d. And Christie's son sold Garrick's pictures in 1823 for a total of £3,504. 13s. 6d., a sum made up in large part by the purchase of four of Hogarth's famous election pictures, for which the architect Sir John Soane paid 1,650 guineas.

The greatest achievement of the founder of Christie's was that he raised the status of both artist and auctioneer. He was himself a connoisseur, an accepted critic – allowing for some hyperbole, perhaps, in his catalogue announcements. Well before his death at the age of 73 he was bringing down his ivory hammer on individual sales of three or even four figures. Behind the mixture of erudition and charm which became manifest once he had an audience about him, was the clever

55

publicist and man of business. He was quick to see the value of advertising in the press. He went further. He was on the board of the *Morning Chronicle,* which started publication in 1769, and of the *Morning Post* which started in 1772, though he left the latter when in 1795 its circulation dropped to 350 copies daily. These papers were read in the coffee houses and clubs very near the Auction Room. He was also a master of what is now called public relations. Once when he had a particularly valuable collection to dispose of he called on the Earl of Chesterfield (the same whose portrait by Gainsborough was praised so rudely by the *Morning Chronicle*). He told his Lordship that he believed he must have seen during his travels some of the pictures now hanging in his auction room. Would his Lordship do him the honour of attending the public view and giving his opinion on them?

Lord Chesterfield was gratified. He talked about the invitation to his friends, and on the appointed day arrived in a carriage and six with numerous attendants. This caused a stir in Pall Mall. Christie showed him round, discussing the pictures with him, while the rest of the audience kept near enough to overhear and store up for repetition the opinions expressed.

Although Christie concentrated more and more on pictures he continued to sell furniture, trinkets, and any article of artistic or curious interest; so it was by no means only picture buyers who thronged his Great Room in Pall Mall to enjoy either as participants or spectators the extraordinary fascination of an auction. In 1795 he sold the jewels of 'La Comtesse Dubarry, deceased' for £8,791. 4s. 9d. But of still greater interest, or curiosity, must have been the announcement that Mr Christie would sell on Thursday, 5 May, 1791 the furniture, swords, jewels and valuable manuscripts of 'the Chevalière *(sic)* d'Eon.' The Chevalier was not yet dead; was to live, in fact, for another nineteen years. But d'Eon's pension had been stopped, and funds had become very short. A sale of old treasures was essential. These personal possessions might have thrown some light on the still unsolved question about d'Eon, particularly interesting in the street where bigger bets were made than anywhere else in London. The auction was written up in every English newspaper. It was a good story – and excellent publicity.

Charles Geneviève Louis Auguste André Timothée d'Eon was born in France in 1710. At the age of three years the child was dressed in girl's clothes and dedicated to the Virgin as Carlotta Geneviève Louise Augusta Timothéa, with Marie added. He went to school as a boy, with a boy's clothes and names, and in due time became a Doctor of Law. As a protégé of Prince Conti he was sent to Russia as a secret agent. There d'Eon wore woman's clothes, and as a woman became a confidante of the Empress. Returning to France, d'Eon was considered to have assisted in the alliance then forming between France, Russia, and Austria, and was rewarded by Louis XV with a grant of money, the title of Chevalier, and the rank of Lieutenant of Dragoons. After other missions to Russia, again as a woman, d'Eon fought bravely with the French army in Germany, being promoted to Captain.

In 1762 he was sent to London as a diplomat. This was the cover for a secret mission to report on the possibilities of invading England. He had been appointed personally by King Louis and was later made plenipotentiary. He is said to have become intolerably conceited, living in tremendous style and running up debts which he expected the French Government to pay.

But the main interest of the English in d'Eon concerned that individual's sex. Bets – 'investments' as they were called – were made to a total of £120,000. There was, of course, one quite simple way of settling the question beyond all doubt, but d'Eon was not co-operative. He even published a warning that he would kill in a duel anyone who attempted the liberty, and he was a good swordsman. Finally what amounted to a test case was brought before Lord Mansfield. The jury decided that 'on the evidence' (which was mainly hearsay) d'Eon was a woman.

Where English law ruled the Chevalier had become the Chevalière. Justice had presumably been done, although it had not been seen to be done. But d'Eon returned to France and presented herself at court in the uniform of a Captain of Hussars. Being commanded to change into woman's clothes she made the excuse – for once literally true – that she had not a thing to wear. So she was fitted out by the court with a splendid trousseau of female clothing and trinkets. When she was asked, some time later, if she did not in matters of honour regret the loss of a sword, she replied that she had done so at first, but had learned that she could achieve as much or more with her slipper.

D'Eon came back to England. She had been granted by the French Government a pension amounting to £500 a year provided that she wore women's clothes. The object of this condition is not known for certain: possibly it was thought that a woman would be less likely to cause political trouble. Five hundred pounds was a sum sufficient to live on. But the French Revolution put a stop to the pension. That was when the swords, jewels, manuscripts, etc., came under Christie's hammer at 83 Pall Mall.

D'Eon, by then 63 years old, made a living by giving fencing displays. By male standards the sword-play was good, by female quite amazing. She continued to draw audiences at Carlton House and elsewhere until one day the button came off her opponent's foil and she was wounded in the armpit. From that wound she never recovered. She was confined to her house and her bed, looked after by an old woman companion, until she died in the year 1810, aged eighty-two.

It being over forty years since an English court of law had ruled that the Chevalier was a woman, people had forgotten all the betting and discussion, and for a long time had ceased to be curious about this old French lady. But the person who laid out the body got a shock. A post-mortem was ordered. The doctor's report was that the breast was remarkably full; the throat was that of a woman; the well-rounded arms, hands and fingers were those of a stout female; the legs and feet corresponded with the arms and hands; but the sexual organs were male and in every respect perfectly formed.

In 1813 James Christie II auctioned at 83 Pall Mall the remainder of the Chevalier's possessions, consisting mainly of books, retaining the corset and certain other relics for his personal interest.

About the time of the first Chevalier d'Eon sale, Christie's pre-views of pictures to be auctioned evolved into evening receptions. The Great Room was brilliantly lighted for the brilliant company. Porters from the Opera, who knew everyone, were posted at the door to keep out undesirables and announce the great. London had never known this type of evening entertainment. Pall Mall led another fashion.

7
Eighteenth-Century Clubs

I T   I S   C O M M O N L Y   S A I D that clubs derived from coffee houses. More accurately, they were a union of coffee house and tavern, or of the amenities which these two offered. We have called the coffee houses unofficial parliaments. Politics is an unsuitable subject for mixed company, not because it is improper, but because in regard to it women tend to appeal to and accept the judgement of men, which destroys the free-for-all stimulus of argument. What is more, they do this not because the subject is above their heads, but because it is beneath their interest.

Coffee houses also provided a haven from the demanding pleasures of domesticity. A man could drink coffee, tea, or chocolate, smoke, cover himself with snuff, bury himself in a newspaper, talk or sit silent, exactly as he felt inclined. But coffee houses did not at first serve meals, and a man must eventually eat. The eighteenth-century taverns of St James's were also masculine havens, *and* they provided excellent food and drink. The deduction was so obvious that it is surprising no-one acted on it before the advent of William Almack.

As to the coffee houses and taverns which did not take each other over, the former evolved into pleasure gardens, which offered quite as much pleasure to ladies as to men, probably more; but these were finally swamped by the spread of urban building. After a thirty year interval they reappeared as tea-shops. The latter changed – one must not say degenerated – into pubs, places for sustaining the spirit with spirits and beer but the flesh with nothing better than a sandwich or meat and two veg. Neither pubs nor teashops took root in later Pall Mall –

until only the other day a seedling of Twining's suddenly appeared.

The club was more than a direct descendant of its two parents. Anyone with decent clothes and enough money in his pocket could enter any coffee house or tavern. Such places tended to be exclusive only because the gregarious human trends towards his own particular flock – social or, especially in the early days, political. But these establishments were governed only by the laws of the land. Clubs made their own rules in addition to those laws. They lived partly, sometimes largely, on the subscriptions paid by members, who were elected either by the whole club or by its committee, its cabinet.

The most general rule was that which excluded women. In the early days there were also some political exclusions. For instance, the original rules of Almack's Society, the precursor of both Brooks's and Boodle's, forbade membership of any other London club, or of 'what is at present called Arthur's or by whatever Name that Society or club may be afterwards called' (it was afterwards called White's). But it was generally found that the procedure of electing a candidate was in itself a sufficient screen. Thus people with a common interest were knotted together like the grain in a wooden club – gamblers and non-gamblers (a small group, this latter, in the early days), Whigs and Tories, later Liberals and Conservatives. There has never been a Labour club in the Pall Mall sense. Plenty of that persuasion could afford it, and they would profit from the opportunity for discussion in comfortable privacy. But they were born too late to enjoy the same advantages as their opponents without seeming to imitate them. However, there are clubs of little or no political bias, to which a good many Socialists belong. Candidates for membership of the most exclusive establishments are asked fewer personal questions than are applicants for a visa for the United States.

Leaving aside predominant interests, which change, the first Pall Mall clubs may conveniently be grouped under two headings: those which were born and died in the Street or died soon after moving, and those which were born there and moved to live elsewhere. Pall Mall has retained no eighteenth-century club, although it was the nursery of two of the most famous.

Those in the first group are the curious ones. They ceased fairly soon because they had no sufficient reason to exist. The originators failed to realise that a club is a business, and a business lives only as long as the need which it supplies. A good example of this group was the Macaroni. It was formed in 1764, and appears to have met at No. 49, one of Almack's two houses on the north side of Pall Mall. Its membership was described by Horace Walpole as 'all the travelled young men who wear long curls and spying glasses'. The Macaronis *(sic)* were rich. They had done the Grand Tour and considered themselves leaders in questions of culture and taste. They went so far as to import macaroni as an exotic dish. But not even spaghetti could keep them together. The club lived for less than ten years.

The term Macaroni, however, continued to be used, with a more and more disapproving significance, for the type of young man who went in for extravagances of dress and behaviour. They were the ones who were 'with it' in those days. Therefore there continued to be Macaronis until the 'squares' grew so tired of their behaviour that they ceased to comment on it. Then the Macaronis ceased.

Before that, a number of the richest and most extravagant (in every sense) had formed another club, the Savoir Vivre. It met in 1772 at the Star and Garter on the south side of Pall Mall and continued there for four years. Meanwhile it was having constructed in St James's Street a clubhouse which should surpass all others in elegance. The cost was over £10,000. In 1776 the members moved in, making themselves comfortable on sofas and chairs covered with satin, in rooms hung with classical pictures and ennobled by statuary. Here, as in the more modest surroundings of the Star and Garter, they wore a uniform of scarlet cloth with a velvet collar and sleeves of *bleu céleste*. They entertained lavishly, first at the Pantheon, and they gambled, says Boswell, to 'a desperate extent'. To maintain their reputation as highly cultured Macaronis they encouraged the arts. The year after the club's inception in Pall Mall the *Gentleman's Magazine* carried this item, 'The Savoir-Vivre Club, at a full meeting resolved that the following premiums be assigned at the first meeting of that club in March 1774, and every succeeding year at the same time and in like manner: 1. A gold medal and a bank note for £100 for the best poem published during the preceding year . . .' and similar prizes for the best oil painting, sculpture, engraving on copper, and musical composition.

What were these young men really like? We will look at a couple of famous members, one an aristocrat, the other a commoner. But before doing so it is only fair to state the truism that clubs, like families, suffer in history because black sheep are always the most noticeable animals in a flock. And since most of us have at least a little black under our sheep's white clothing they seem the most interesting.

Thomas, second Baron Lyttleton, was called 'the wicked Lord Lyttleton'. It sounds like the title of a novelette, and his life might be the theme of one. He was a model boy, handsome and accomplished. He read Milton with ecstatic pleasure and painted so well that Mrs Montagu, the bluest blue-stocking, said that he combined the excellencies of Claude and Salvator Rosa. He was educated at Eton and Oxford. While an undergraduate he became engaged to the charming daughter of a General. Then he went to France and Italy for two years, and – we read – practised the fashionable vices. Practice makes perfect in bad as well as good; his engagement dissolved. He returned to England, entered Parliament, and married someone else. A contemporary writer described his early married life. 'He has lived for the last two months with only laying at home now and then, at the gaming tables, at the Savoir Vivre and with women.'

64

11   A sale at Christie's Auction Room. Cartoon by Rowlandson

. . . and 42

12   Chevalier d'Eon at the age of 25

He held the philosophy that our actions are ordained, not voluntary. But he was not beyond remorse. He published some highly moral verses in honour of his wife. He then left her and went to Paris with a barmaid. He was, in fact, a typical rake. One thing not generally appreciated about our disreputable forefathers is the energy which they possessed. Temperate living, scientific feeding, all the money which goes into education, should have made us capable of a greater mental and physical output than they. But it has not worked out like that. Lyttleton returned to England when his father died. He was by no means a reformed character, but parallel with his dissipations he carried on an active life in the House of Lords, becoming a Privy Councillor in 1775.

As a rake, Lyttleton was in the same class as Charles James Fox. Charles Graves in his *Leather Armchairs* records how Fox once gambled without a break from one evening until the next afternoon, his fortune changing from £12,000 up to £11,000 down. (The strain on the nerves must be considered.) Next day he made a speech in the House of Commons on the Thirty-Nine Articles. That night he dined at Brooks's at 11.30. He then went to White's and drank until 7 a.m. He moved on to Almack's, where he won £6,000 at cards before starting for Newmarket in the afternoon. The question at issue is not whether one would have enjoyed such crowded days and nights, but whether one would still have been upright on arrival at Newmarket and capable of distinguishing a horse from an hallucination.

On the night of 24/25 November 1779 Lord Lyttleton dreamed that a bird flew in at his window, and transformed itself into a woman who told him that he would be dead within three days. Next day he made a vigorous speech in the Lords on the condition of Ireland. To his friends he recounted his dream, affecting to take it lightly. But the story was at once on everybody's lips, and one may be sure that he was closely watched. For two days the sharpest eyes could see nothing in any way wrong with him, and nothing of interest occurred. On the third morning, feeling very well, he said that he would 'bilk the ghost'. During the day, walking with his cousin, Hugh Fortescue, he passed a graveyard and remarked on the number of 'vulgar fellows' who had died at thirty-five, his own age. 'But you and I who are gentlemen,' he said, 'shall live to a ripe old age.'

He dined that night in Epsom and passed a cheerful evening. He got home at about eleven o'clock. He died as soon as he got into bed. His manservant, who was with him, said that death was instantaneous.

The commoner-member to be described is Richard Smith. He was very much a commoner. 'This insolent man's father', says William Hickey, 'kept a little cheesemonger's shop in Jermyn Street, St James's Market.' As a boy Smith was 'a sad profligate scapegrace'. To get him out of harm's way his father sent him to India, where he became General in charge of the East India Company's army in Bengal and amassed a huge fortune, with which he returned to England. The climate and his experiences had not improved him. He 'betrayed an insolent superiority and superciliousness that offended everybody.'

It is understandable that a self-made man might want to get into the fashionable Savoir Vivre. It is much harder to guess why the club elected him. Perhaps he amused them. At any rate he won the reputation of being the biggest gambler of them all, and he seems to have been an instigator of the building of the new and magnificent club house in St James's Street. Going into politics, he was twice elected M.P. for Hinton. On the first occasion the election was declared void, and on the second (in 1776) he was sentenced to six months' imprisonment and a heavy fine for gross bribery and corruption. In 1779 he was elected a member of Brooks's.

In 1782 the Savoir Vivre finally proved that it did not know how to live. Its splendid building was sold to Boodle's, which moved in in the following year and has been there ever since.

Another short-lived club which yet made a considerable reputation for itself was Goostree's, 51 Pall Mall. (The proprietor's name was James Goostree.) It had a small but select membership of young men, most of whom had been contemporaries at the University and had just started public life together. The history of the club shows how in fourteen years they grew from foolishness to wisdom.

Goosetree's started in 1773. Pitt seems to have been the instigator. In one of his letters George Selwyn wrote, 'Young Pitt has formed a society of young Ministers who are to fight under his banner, and these are the Duke of Rutland, Mr Banks, Lord Chatham, etc., etc., and they assemble at Goostree's.' At first there was a good deal of gambling, Pitt joining in with the intensity of concentration which he applied to everything he did. But later, quite suddenly, he gave it up altogether. The other members followed his lead, and the club acquired the almost unique reputation of one in which there was no gaming. As such it came to an end when Goostree sold the house by auction at Christie's. It is of interest in the later development of Pall Mall in that it was bought by a bookseller. But the house, long since demolished, must have had gambling in its mortar, for Goostree had acquired it from General John Scott. Selwyn often mentioned Scott as a dedicated and successful card player. From what one hears of him he was a most *simpatico* gambler. The *Gentleman's Magazine*, for instance, told this anecdote:

'Being one night at Stapleton's when a messenger brought him the news of his Lady being delivered of a daughter, he turned about to the company, "You see, Gentlemen (says he), I must be under the necessity of doubling my stakes in order to make a fortune for the girl." He accordingly played rather deeper than usual, the consequence of which was, he found himself, after a few hours play, a loser of £8,000. This gave occasion for some of the company to rally the General on his *daughter's fortune*; but the other, who had an evenness of temper that nothing could warp, and a judgement in play superior to most, told them he had still a dependence on the luck of the night; and, to make his word good, he accordingly played on – when, about 7 o'clock in the morning, besides his £8,000, he brought home £15,000.'

When this baby, Joan, grew up and married she was worth £100,000, and her sister inherited an equal fortune. For General Scott, the cards brought in money. He played seriously. While others went to the green-baize-covered table fuddled with wine and heavy with too much food, Scott, who had dined on cold chicken and toast with only water to drink, sat down clear-headed. He had besides a photographic memory, and his favourite game was whist. It is interesting that his fellow players, whom he must have fleeced of well over the £200,000 he left, bore him no ill will. He was a very popular man.

Before leaving the subject of gambling it is worth considering the sums which changed hands every night in the clubs of St James's. Money was, of course, worth much more then than now. Consider the prices of property. The palatial house built for the Savoir Vivre cost £10,000, a sum so large that it was commented upon as an extravagance. Yet it was less than Charles James Fox lost and won in the course of a single sitting. Scott's £15,000 win should be measured against the sum received by Goostree when he re-sold the house which he had bought from him: £2,047. In the last chapter, speaking of the prices bid for pictures at Christie's, it was remarked that a gentleman would pay more for a horse than an Old Master. Even horses came far behind the excitement of a game of chance. Those dignified, unworried days! Men must have had something nagging at their nerves to make them buy distraction at such a price.

We turn with relief to a society where nothing of that kind went on. For two years, between December 1769 and December 1771, there was in one of Almack's houses on the north side of

Pall Mall a club which admitted ladies on equal terms with men – or rather men on equal terms with ladies. It was called the Ladies' Club, or Coterie. Election was by ballot, but with the proviso that men could vote only for ladies, and ladies only for men. Thus the members had no control over the election or exclusion of those of their own sex; but could show approval or dislike of the other. The intended significance of this is nowhere explained. It might have provided the means of getting over an apocryphal rule attributed to a present-day club: 'Members may not bring their mistresses to the club unless they be the wives of other members.' But this cannot have been the case with the Coterie. An anonymous lady thus described its objects: 'Instead of midnight revels, this assembly should meet before the noon of day, with spirits unimpaired by nocturnal parties; no natural rest destroyed by lack of innocence or fortune at masquerade or gaming tables.'

The Rules of the club included the following: 'That dinner be on the table by half after 4 o'clock exactly, and that every member present shall pay 8 shillings, exclusive of wine, which the men are to pay. (The men, it may be observed, retained their privilege of paying.)

'That no foreigner shall be allowed to pay an annual subscription. (This was five guineas.)

'That supper shall be on the table at 11 o'clock exactly. (The price was left blank.)

'No play in the eating room on penalty of paying the whole bill.'

Much time was spent in edifying conversation, but after dinner the members played loo, a card game whose rules are still included in a modern encyclopaedia.

The Coterie was probably the most aristocratic club that has ever existed. Among 123 elected members were five dukes, five duchesses, twenty-three lords and their ladies. The club moved from Pall Mall to Wildman's in Albemarle Street; but it did not last long. It died of exclusiveness. The proprietor, James

Cullen, was left heavily in debt.

Having dealt with these short-lived clubs we may turn to the antecedents and early years of two which are still very much alive. Mention has more than once been made to William Almack. He was to the clubs of St James's what the Earl of St Albans had been to St James's as a whole. There is considerable doubt about his origin. He has been described as a Scotsman whose real name was MacCaul, but who changed it to Almack because the English found it easier to pronounce. That is far-fetched and unsubstantiated. There are more grounds for believing that he was of a Yorkshire Quaker family, though his chosen profession was scarcely suitable for a Quaker. Almost certainly he was at first a valet to the Duke of Hamilton in whose London house he met his Scottish wife, who was maid to the Duchess.

One pictures Almack as being as infallible as Jeeves, knowing exactly how to deal with gentlemen drunk or sober, and besides that as a shrewd business man who planned ahead and chose his associates or employees with unerring judgement.

During the latter half of the 1750s Almack ran a tavern in Curzon Street. By 1760 he was established in No. 49 Pall Mall, and two years later had acquired from General John Scott the lease of No. 50. The first-mentioned of these two houses was for five years a licensed tavern; the second he at once launched as a private society. In fact it was a club, the members of which paid an annual subscription of two guineas and observed rules similar to those of a present-day club. In return they could find all the newspapers at No. 50 and could eat and drink at fixed prices – eight shillings for dinner, six for supper, with port at half-a-crown a bottle. Almack's assistants or partners were Brooks, Ellis, and Boodle. Between them they soon won a high reputation for comfort and good food.

No. 49 remained a tavern until 1764, when it became Almack's Club. It was so called until 1778, when it removed to St James's Street under the management and name of William

Brooks. Brooks's Club has not moved since then. The other club was managed by Edward Boodle, and took his name. As already mentioned, it transferred in 1783 to the house in St James's Street which had been built for the Savoir Vivre.

Thus Pall Mall sent round the corner the two great clubs it had nursed. But the next century was to see the birth of a much larger generation.

8
Beau Astley and a Loud Quack

BEFORE GAINSBOROUGH CAME to the western wing of Schomberg House the whole building had belonged to John Astley. He was one of those people of whom few are fond, but among those few is Fortune.

He was born at Wem in Shropshire in 1730. He studied painting, and at the age of nineteen managed to scrape together enough money to visit Rome. We know two facts about him there. The first is that he became indebted to Reynolds in the sum of £12. 15s. 6d.; the second, which also suggests poverty, concerns his invitation to a party. It was a warm evening and the gentlemen took off their coats. Astley was reluctant to follow their example. When he did so it was seen that the back of his waistcoat consisted of a canvas with a waterfall painted on it. He returned penniless to London, and met Horace Walpole, who for some reason took a fancy to this 'clever, conceited, out-at-elbows, and reckless fellow.' Walpole gave him his patronage until Astley went off to try his luck in Ireland: not a land to which those in search of fortune generally go.

Of his skill as an artist Samuel Redgrave says, 'He had much talent, particularly in portraits. His colouring was agreeable . . . but the finish slight, the character and expression weak.' He became one of the sights of the town for the ladies of Dublin, for when they sat for their portraits he used his sword as a maulstick. It is difficult to imagine a more unsuitable substitute. In three years he made three thousand pounds. With what remained of that – probably not much – he set off for

London again. On a whim he turned aside to visit his birth-place. There he met a rich widow named Lady Dunkerfield Daniell. She sat for him, married him within a week, and settled on him the Table estate which brought him in £1,000 a year. She lived just long enough to make a new will by which the Dunkerfield estate, worth £5,000 a year, was to go to her daughter for life and thereafter to Astley if he should still be alive.

In London, Astley gained the reputation of 'a gasconading spendthrift and a beau of the flashiest order'. He bought Schomberg House for £5,000 from Lord Holderness. Directly after accepting Astley's offer Holderness was bid £7,000 for the house, but kept to his earlier bargain. Beau Astley spent a further £5,000 on the house, dividing it into three, and building on the top of the central portion, which he occupied, a studio which gave a view over the Surrey hills.

He was soon reduced to poverty. Then Lady Daniell's daughter died and the Dunkerfield estate went to him. He married again, speculated in a colliery, and lost all he had except his houses. Then his brother, a surgeon at Putney, died and left him £10,000.

It was after Astley had gone to end his days in penitence and fear of poverty at Dunkerfield Lodge that Gainsborough rented the western wing of Schomberg House. A few years later there moved into Astley's house a still stranger individual.

Dr James Graham studied medicine at Edinburgh University but did not qualify. In his late twenties he went to America, but soon returned to England. Then, after a few years in Bath, he came to London, where he practised first in the Adelphi and then in Schomberg House. The first of these London consulting rooms he called the Temple of Health, the second the Temple of Health and Hymen. The actual temple was Astley's view-point studio.

At first he concentrated upon the cure of deafness and blind-ness – prosaic work compared with what was to follow. Yet even here his skill as a publicist and his pseudo-poetic twist of mind were evident. He published a little book addressed to 'The Inhabitants of Great Britain, particularly to those residing in the great Metropolis' which contained numerous letters of praise and gratitude. The following, which might have been taken from the testimonial of a patent medicine today, is typical:

Sir:

After having been afflicted with extreme deafness and noise in both ears for a long time, I thus publicly declare the speedy and complete cure of both I have received at your hands. I wish to express my gratitude and joy, but cannot find words adequate to utter.

One patient wrote a rhymed acrostic:

Deign to accept the tribute which I owe

One grateful, trembling tear permit to flow;

Can I be silent when such hopes are given,

T'enjoy my sight, the first best gift of heav'n?

O Muse descend! in most exalted lays,

Replete with softest notes, attend his praise.

The lines of the second verse start with the letters of Graham, concluding with a comparison with God:

Arm'd by the Deity with pow'r divine,

Mortals revere His attributes in *thine!*

Tempting though it is to believe that Graham wrote this himself, I believe that most of the testimonials are genuine.

Graham's cures always appear to have had some medical sense in them, but to have been more or less flavoured with the occult. He called himself at first an occultist and aurist. Later he worked in, and finally worked upon, the very human desire to be a fine physical specimen. In the ante-room of the Temple of Health the patient or visitor found a pile of discarded crutches, and he was then ushered to the first floor by gigantic footmen. Here music was played, and statues showed what humanity ought to look like. Highly decorated apparatus, including an electrical throne (which had cost, it was pointed out, over £10,000) was displayed as the means of achieving physical perfection. The cures were all 'natural'. Mud baths were advocated. Sir Walter Scott in his youth, trying to be rid of his lameness, was one of Graham's patients.

In the Temple of Health and Hymen in Pall Mall Graham added yet another appeal, certainly no less sure. He gave a daily lecture on 'The generation, increase and improvement of the Human Species'. It began by advocating selective breeding, with a delicate exposition on the facts of life. 'Yes, gentlemen! The complete future child (like the plant with its leaves, flowers, fruits and seeds, wrapped up invisibly in the seed) actually subsists in a dormant or inanimate state . . .' He never used a nasty word in his lectures. To tell the truth they make heavy reading, but they are masterpieces of suggestion. And, in fact, not very much was left to the imagination, for there was plenty actually to be seen. The 'rosy, athletic and truly gigantic goddess of Health and Hymen' was exhibited on 'the celestial throne'. Modern Soho lacks the frank and direct appeal of Schomberg House in the days of Dr Graham's strip without tease. Crowds of rowdy persons are said to have attended the lectures, and there were imputations that the police had been bribed not to interfere. One wonders how his next-door neighbour, Gainsborough, reacted to all this.

Married couples who wanted to make certain of having perfect children could hire the Grand Celestial State Bed at £50 a night. It was twice the size of an ordinary double bed, twelve feet long and nine feet wide. 'It is supported by forty pillars of brilliant glass of great strength and of most excellent workman-ship . . . sweetly delicate . . . They are moreover invisibly encrusted with a certain transparent varnish, in order to render the insulation still more complete . . . We may have even in the most unfavourable weather abundance of electrical fire.

'The sublime, magnificent and, I may say, the super-celestial doom [sic] of the bed which contains the odiferous, balmy and ethereal spices, odours, and essences, and which is the grand magazine or reservoir of those vivifying and invigorating influences which are exhaled and dispersed by the breath of the music, and by the attenuating, repelling and accelerating force of the electrical fire, is very curiously inlaid . . . with brilliant plates of looking glass, so disposed as to reflect the various charms and attitudes of the happy couple who repose in the bed in the most flattering, most luxurious and most enchanting style.'

Dr Graham goes on to describe the pictures, painted under the dome of the bed, of the marriage of Cupid and Psyche with a figure of Hymen behind, holding aloft a torch flaming with electric fire, and above all 'a pair of real-living turtle-doves who, on a little bed of roses, coo and bill under the super-animating influences of the genial fire.'

Elsewhere about the dome (it is not clear how they were fitted in) were groups of nymphs and graces with musical instruments in their hands, 'which by the exquisite and most expensive mechanism are made to breathe forth sounds'. The posts of the bed were likewise musical. 'In sweet concert with the other instruments, at the commencement of the tender dalliances . . . (they) breathe forth celestial sounds lulling them to visions of elysian joys '

The sheets were nothing so coarse as linen. They were of silk or satin in various colours, 'suited to the complexion of the lady who is to repose on them, pale green, for example, rose colour or sky blue . . . and sweetly perfumed in the oriental manner'. The mattress was stuffed with the hair of English stallions 'procured at vast expense'.

But the chief principle of the bed was scientific. 'About fifteen hundred pounds weight of artificial and compound magnets are so disposed and arranged as to be continually pouring forth in an ever-flowing circle inconceivable and irresistibly powerful tides of the magnetic effluvium, which every philosophical gentleman knows has a very strong affinity with the electric fire. These magnets, too, being pressed, give that charming springyness – that sweet undulating, titillating, vibratory, soul-dissolving, marrow-melting motion . . .'

The detailed description of the bed is continued in another thousand words or more. But the reader probably already has a sufficiently clear picture of this enormous and highly intricate piece of furniture.

Pall Mall put up with Dr Graham until his property was seized for debt. Only then did he leave, of his own accord, having somehow managed to buy back most of his apparatus. Written accounts convey little of the personality which is the real secret of success, or at least of toleration.

Graham was a very curious person, more than a mere quack. For instance, his rules of diet and behaviour would be approved by many authorities today. He preached that meat should be excluded from the diet, that stimulants should be taken most sparingly, that one should sleep hard with open windows and few coverings. Perhaps he went too far in forbidding his patients to wear woollen clothes. He himself wore a linen suit and black silk stockings. He was a keen advocate of cold baths. In one of his publications is the case history of a lady who came to him because she could not have a child. He prescribed a cold shower several times a night. She at first demurred; but the treatment was effective.

He issued about twenty books and pamphlets, which record his movements and governing interests after leaving Pall Mall. 'A Treatise on the All-Cleansing, All-Healing, and All-Invigorating Qualities of Simple Earth', was first published in London and then in a quite different form in Newcastle-upon-Tyne. The *Dictionary of National Biography* quotes from *Notes and Queries*, 1791, a description of how Graham and a young lady 'stripped into their first suits and were each interred up to the chin, their heads beautifully dressed and powdered, appearing not unlike two full-grown cauliflowers.'

Graham continued to travel and lecture – with or without

permission – in Scotland, England, France, the Isle of Man, Ireland. But he returned finally to the town where he had been born and educated. There this strange man, who had once claimed that he could prolong life to at least a hundred and fifty years, died suddenly at the age of forty-nine.

13   Old and New Schomberg House

14   'Gas in Pall Mall.' Cartoon by Rowlandson

9
Carlton House and the National Gallery

UNTIL THE FIRST QUARTER of the nineteenth century had passed the only direct roads from Piccadilly to Pall Mall were St James's Street and Haymarket, the western and eastern limits of St Alban's Quadrilateral. The observant reader will notice that something is missing: Piccadilly Circus and that part of Regent Street to the south of it. They did not exist – nor did any of Regent Street for that matter. In that part of the area a great change took place about that time, although the rest of the street plan has hardly changed at all since the 1660s.

If the reader, standing in Piccadilly Circus, were carried back in time to the first quarter of the nineteenth century – not so long ago – he would have no notion where he was, except that he was somewhere in Piccadilly. Let him ask the shortest way to Pall Mall and he would be directed as follows: 'That passage, Eagle Street, will take you to Jermyn Street. Turn to the left along it until you can turn right down Market Street. Leave St James's Market on your left. Beyond the market you will find St Albans Street, which runs straight down to Pall Mall.' Strange streets (except for Jermyn Street) flanked by buildings he has never seen; and having reached Pall Mall he is faced by an enormous house which overlaps the site of what he knows today as the United Service Club, Waterloo Place and the Athenaeum. This was Carlton House – Carlton Palace, as it had come to be called. It had cost over a million pounds, a vast fortune at that time. Nothing of it remains to be seen today –

except some pillars and the portico removed to Trafalgar Square.

Carlton House took its name from Baron Carleton, *né* Henry Boyle, who received it from the king at the beginning of the eighteenth century. In comparison with its later size and form it was then a poor place. But when Carleton died, 'holding the fair Duchess (of Marlborough) by the hand, and being fed at the same time with a fat chicken' – according to Lady Mary Wortley Montagu – it passed to Lord Burlington, and thence, via his mother and Lord Chesterfield (as trustee), to Frederick Louis, Prince of Wales, son of George II and father of George III. Thus it fell into the hands of the Hanoverians.

Frederick Louis, according to Lady Mary Wortley Montagu, was a man of grace and charm. But it is only a mother who really appreciates her child, and Frederick Louis's mother said of him, 'My dear first born is the greatest ass, and the greatest liar, and the greatest *canaille,* and the greatest beast in the whole world, and I heartily wish he was out of it.' Unlike most mothers' wishes, this was of the kind which comes true in the end. Frederick Louis died in 1751, by which time his mother was already dead, but it is to be hoped she slept more happily in her grave thereafter. Frederick Louis's widow added to Carlton House the home of George Bubb Dodington, which was the next building to the west along Pall Mall. After her death Carlton House was occupied in 1783 by the next Prince of Wales, he who eventually became George IV.

Eventually – but meanwhile the money flowed. The Prince, with the help of Henry Holland, John Nash, and other architects, began a series of alterations and enlargements which continued well into the next century. In 1787 Parliament voted £20,000 for the completion of the house, not knowing that twice that sum had already been spent on it. On top of that the Prince of Wales bought thirteen houses in order to extend his Pall Mall frontage. He had installed Mrs Fitzherbert in Carlton House, following his formal marriage to her, but she was not the cause of his extravagance. When in 1795 his debts had risen to £639,890 he felt compelled to make a bargain with his father, the King. This cost him something, for his dislike of his father was equalled only by his father's dislike of him. But the bones of the bargain which they came to was that he, George Prince of Wales, agreed to marry Caroline, Princess of Brunswick – that was what father wanted – and that he in exchange received what he needed: the settlement of his debts and a further £26,000.

He had not seen Princess Caroline, only a painting of her. When she arrived he stared, kissed her on the cheek without a word, then retired to a corner of the room and drank a glass of brandy. It was a discouraging start, and the bargain did not work out. The marriage was soon on the rocks and George in debt again. Princess Caroline went to live at Blackheath, and Mrs Fitzherbert returned to Carlton House.

The passing of the Regency Bill in 1811 was the occasion for the biggest party that even Carlton House had ever seen. Then came the Treaty of Paris, and another party. Then a fête to the Duke of Wellington. One way and another, in the five years following the Regency Bill, Carlton House cost another £160,000. When the taxpayers learnt of this they were unfavourably impressed. If Britain had had any more of those Georges she would soon have had no more Kings.

During these latter years John Nash had become the Prince Regent's favourite architect, continually occupied on some addition or improvement to Carlton House. Having won the royal patronage, Nash proposed his fondest and longest nurtured scheme – to bring a fine new street sweeping southwards from Regent's Park to the doors of Carlton House. The prospect of this access of grandeur appealed to the Regent and was duly approved by Parliament. But Nash's 'New Street' did not fulfil its first intention. Long before the work had been completed George had become interested in the future of Buckingham Palace and taken a dislike to Carlton House. By

1829 it had been demolished.

Thus the great thoroughfare which, using the modern names, started in Regent's Park and ran as Portland Place and Upper Regent Street to Oxford Circus, thence to Piccadilly Circus and beyond it – at the expense of St James's Market, St Albans Street and numerous houses – ended in the anticlimax of rubble. But, quite incidentally, something of great importance had been done. St Albans's self-contained *faubourg* had been considerably opened up.

Less than twenty years later an attempt was made to open it up still more. Nash, among his many other royal commissions, was architect of Buckingham Palace in its original form. He planned for it a most imposing entrance, an archway of white limestone modelled on Rome's Arch of Constantine. It was erected. But it was not right. Nobody liked it there, least of all Parliament, which had been tricked into building a palace when it thought it was voting money for no more than the refurbishing of Buckingham House. So the nation found itself with what looked like a particularly large white elephant on its hands. What to do with it: A suggestion was seriously canvassed to place it on an extension of Pall Mall, or a widened Cleveland Row, as an extrance to Green Park. This idea was first put forward in a letter signed by 'A Wiltshireman' which was published in *The Builder* on 11 November 1848.

I hear it is reported that Mr Pennethorne recommends the erection of a new National Gallery on the site of Cleveland-row, St James's, and to raise the present building in Trafalgar Square a storey and make it fit for what it was originally intended, viz, the *atelier* of the Royal Academy of Painting. I do not pretend to be a competent judge of the eligibility of the proposed site for a National Gallery, but what I wish to recommend is, that the front of the new building should be set back so as to stand in line with the north side of Pall Mall (which is really a fine-looking street with a very ill-looking western termination), and thus make an opening into the

Green-park, and remove the marble arch from Buckingham Palace to that site, which, I humbly think, would be a very appropriate one, in more respects than one, and afford a beautiful vista down the whole length of Pall Mall.

The proposal received considerable publicity, and was later revived by the architect Barry. But it finally died. The marble arch was erected at Marble Arch and the National Gallery remained on its present site, with the pillars and portico of Carlton House included in the structure. But we must now go back a little to tell of the founding of the National Gallery.

The Royal Academy, it will be remembered, provided on its creation a permanent collection of pictures in addition to the annual exhibitions. Sir Joshua Reynolds had felt very strongly that the opportunities for study and comparison which this addition offered were essential for the schooling of British art. But even when it became evident that such a collection, if it were created on a proper scale, would have to be separate from the Academy, there was more talk than action for many years. There were some who were actively hostile to the idea. As great a painter as Constable wrote to a friend in 1822: 'Should there be a National Gallery (which is talked of) there will be an end of the art in poor old England, and she will become, in all that relates to painting, as much a nonentity as every other country that has one. The reason is plain; the manufacturers of pictures are then made the criterion of perfection, instead of Nature.'

In *The Making of the National Gallery* Sir Charles Holmes and C. H. Collins Baker gave one reason for this pessimistic prophecy. So little at that time was known about cleaning pictures, and keeping them clean, that those of any age in London were ingrained with deposits of the dirty air as well as obscured by old varnish: they were as far from their original appearance as is a cobwebbed and dirty bottle of ancient vintage, and the danger lay in artists thinking that this was how good pictures ought to look. In any case no action was taken until the Royal Academy had been proving its value for nearly half a century.

It was a merchant of Russian birth who finally provided the nucleus on which the national collection was formed. Not only for this reason, but because John Julius Angerstein was a man of character and achievement, and a resident in Pall Mall for a dozen years, he must take his place in this story.

He was born at St Petersburg in 1735 and emigrated to England at the age of fifteen. Six years later he became an underwriter at Lloyds. All the business of the greatest insurance organization in the world was at that time still centred on the old coffee house of that name. To anticipate a little, it was through Angerstein's exertions and personal influence that Lloyds as we know it was organized.

While he was still living he was mentioned in *Percy's Anecdotes*, 1821, a sort of *Who's Who* and *Who Was Who* combined, restricted to people of religious or social merit, and written by Sholto and Reuben, two brothers of the Benedictine Monastery of Mont Benger. There are twenty volumes of it. Describing Angerstein's early days as an underwriter the brothers say, 'When his name appeared on a policy, it was sufficient recommendation for the others to follow where he led, without further examination; accordingly other underwriters were eager to see policies sanctioned by his subscription, which speedily acquired so great an authority that for some years after, by way of distinction, they were called Julians.'

In the late eighteenth century, and possible earlier too, the owners of ships which had acquired a bad reputation for seaworthiness, and consequently were expensive or impossible to insure, developed the habit of changing the name of the vessel and submitting the new name to Lloyds. On Angerstein's strong recommendation Parliament passed an Act forbidding the changing of a vessel's name. Another of his suggestions to Parliament was that of a State lottery. He became head of some of the greatest trading firms in the country and amassed a mighty fortune. With this he retired to his house in Pall Mall and used 'the weight of his name and the powers of his active and ready mind' for charitable and useful ends. Of the former the Benedictines said, 'There is not a public charity in the metropolis, nor a national institution of any importance, that is not largely indebted to the princely munificence of John Julius Angerstein, Esq.' One such action was his rescue from bankruptcy of the Veterinary College.

Under the heading of useful comes his suggestion to Lloyds that they should offer a reward of £2,000 for the invention of an unsinkable lifeboat. He also became a sponsor of the detection and punishment of crime. In the 1790s there was at large in London a man who made numerous attacks on what the newspapers called 'the most beautiful part of creation'. Young women returning home at night unattended were assaulted by this man with indecent words, had their clothes torn, and were struck a heavy blow on the left hip. He became known as the Monster. Several of these attacks were made within a few hundred yards of Angerstein's Pall Mall house. He offered a reward of £100 for the Monster's capture and conviction. Various descriptions were given. The Monster was six feet tall, thin-faced, marked by the smallpox. His hair was plaited behind and frizzed at the side. On different occasions he had been seen to carry a stick, a dagger, and a nosegay.

The search was complicated by anonymous letters which stated that the Monster was a highly respected person named Thyckness. He cleared himself, and the mystery continued for months, filling the newspapers. Finally he was arrested (his name was Renwick Williams), tried at the Old Bailey, and given seven years imprisonment. In the course of the trial there never appeared any doubt about his guilt, but the jury only reached their verdict by a majority of two. The Monster had won a certain amount of public sympathy.

Nothing in Angerstein's life so far – except of course the building of his fortune – had been in any way concerned with the future National Gallery. But the point to stress about

Angerstein was his many-sidedness. The collection of pictures was only one of many occupations of his retirement. He set about this last, however, in a most businesslike way. Depending greatly on the advice of his friend, Sir Thomas Lawrence, he filled the living rooms of No. 100 Pall Mall with pictures. There cannot have been much bare wall visible, for some of Angerstein's acquisitions were enormous. The 'Christ raising Lazarus' of Sebastian Piombo is $13\frac{1}{2}$ ft. by $7\frac{1}{2}$ ft. Others of his pictures which are well known are Claude's 'The Embarcation of the Queen of Sheba', and Hogarth's 'Marriage à la Mode'; and, among those which ought to be well known, works by Titian, Rubens, Rembrandt and Poussin.

When Angerstein died in 1823, George Agar Ellis, the future Lord Dover, warned Parliament that the pictures would be sold within a year and urged that they should not be allowed to leave the country. In the same context he mentioned that Sir George Beaumont had promised his own considerable collection to the nation as soon as the Government should find a suitable building to house a National Gallery.

The Prime Minister, Lord Liverpool, was at the time deeply preoccupied with one of the periodic crises of the economy which those of us who know too little history think of as peculiar to our own age. The long, expensive war against Napoleon's France had left a legacy of hamstrung trade, unemployment and unrest. But Parliament was induced to vote £60,000, with which thirty-eight of the Angerstein pictures were bought, and No. 100 Pall Mall was taken over as a National Gallery. Therefore Sir George Beaumont's pictures were added to the collection, and also – somewhat later – those of the Reverend W. Holwell Carr, who had made a similar promise.

The owner of and responsible authority for the pictures was the Treasury, which had provided the money. They appointed a Keeper, William Seguier, a dealer and restorer by profession. They also appointed a Committee of six Gentlemen, later increased to eight, to keep an eye on the Keeper. This committee, which included the Prime Minister, the Chancellor of the Exchequer and the President of the Royal Academy, was in fact the first Board of Trustees.

It is a little difficult to picture the first National Gallery as it stood on the south side of Pall Mall, for it and its neighbouring buildings have all been replaced, and Carlton Gardens, which now separate the Reform Club from 'No. 100', did not exist. More or less in its place was Pall Mall Court, a narrow passage just to the west of the gallery. No. 100 was a large, three-storey building with a frontage on Pall Mall of thirty-three feet and a depth of forty-six. But it was soon not large enough for the collection, which, once it was in existence, soon grew from bequests and purchases. For instance, a group of Constable's admirers presented *The Cornfield* (so he was soon represented in the Gallery which would 'be an end of the art in poor old England'); and Titian's *Bacchus and Ariadne* was bought, with Caracci's *Domine, quo vadis?* and Poussin's *Bacchanalian Dance* included in the £9,000 purchase price.

There were no displays of artistic emotion like those which attended the birth of the Royal Academy, but the young National Gallery had troubles of another sort. Within four years the trustees were complaining to the Treasury that they had no more suitable wall space for pictures and that as a result potential bequeathers might decide not to bequeath.

The Treasury suggested building additional rooms on to No. 100. But this remedy was almost immediately frustrated. During the enlargement of Pall Mall Court to make Carlton Gardens the foundations of the Gallery were undermined and the building became unsafe. So the pictures were moved to No. 105, a house where Mrs Fitzherbert had lived and which had been an annexe of Carlton House. This was only suitable as a temporary home. The Treasury had to put its hand in its pocket again and build the National Gallery on the north side of Trafalgar Square. The National Gallery opened to the public in its third and final home in 1838.

The Treasury may seem too impersonal and business-minded a body to look after the nation's richest store of art. But from the first they behaved as human beings over the National Gallery. When Sir George Beaumont kept his promise and gave his whole collection he found his house empty without it. In particular he felt he could not live without one of his smaller Claude's (No. 61 at the National Gallery). It was returned to him for his lifetime.

10
Gas and the Carlton Club

In 1830 the tories, having been decisively beaten in the General Election, set about the reorganization of their party as a matter of urgency. The first need as they saw it was for a headquarters and place of meeting. No available house being found suitable they decided upon building a club. The site finally chosen was that comprising 92–95 Pall Mall, on the corner of that street and Pall Mall Court, now Carlton Gardens. In these former houses much had happened, and whether or not one holds the metaphysical opinion that from the past of a place emanates something which affects the present, the antecedents of the Carlton Club building in Pall Mall are interesting enough to be examined in some detail.

Some of it we already know. The Star and Garter of the Byron duel, of the Society of Dilettanti and the early Savoir Vivre occupied it in 1794–95. It came to an end at the turn of the century. No. 93 was from 1777 until 1809 part of the site of the Royal Hotel which offered accommodation for 'gentlemen and families of distinction'. This, the only attempt to practise the hotel business in Pall Mall until Cesar Ritz launched the Carlton Hotel, ceased when the proprietor went bankrupt. Thereafter Nos. 93–95 were the site of an experiment in industrial chemistry.

To explain this surprising use of Pall Mall a brief introduction is necessary. In 1763 there had been born in Brunswick a certain Fredrich Albrecht Winzler. Educated in Hamburg, he showed no particular academic ability, but his moral qualities – tireless energy, inflexible obstinacy, and a capacity for infectious enthusiasm – encompassed in a remarkably thick skin – made him adopt as his profession what would now be described as company promoting. Looking about for companies to promote, he visited Paris. Here the chemist, Le Bon, who in 1799 had obtained a patent for his method of producing coal gas, was trying to induce his countrymen to use gas for street lighting. In those restless years which followed the Revolution he could find no one to back him. But Winzler at once saw the potentialities of the discovery. He tried to induce Le Bon to sell him one of his 'thermo lamps'. This the chemist refused to do. But while hungrily following him around as a young bird follows its mother, Winzler picked up enough technical information to exploit the new form of lighting on his own. He could not do this in France because of Le Bon's patent. He came to London, took 93 Pall Mall, and began by pamphlets and lectures to publicize the idea of street lighting by gas. Later, when he started to demonstrate, he took over 94 and 95 as well. By this time he had changed his name to Frederick Albert Winsor to reduce the automatic resistance of the English to anything foreign.

Coal gas had, in fact, already been produced in Britain. Lord Dundonald had made it on his Scottish estate in 1780 – to amuse his friends. He saw no practical use for it, only for the by-products. Another Scotsman, William Murdoch, had made it for the use of his firm, Boulton & Watt, in their Birmingham factory. Yet Winsor's proposition was startlingly new, because he saw much further than anybody else. When no one had yet thought of carrying gas from one house to another he proposed lighting the whole of London, the whole of England even, with coal gas carried in pipes. As a start he set up furnaces and retorts in his Pall Mall houses.

His early lectures at the Lyceum Theatre were not entirely successful. He did not speak English well enough to deliver them himself, and so depended on an interpreter to read them. Sometimes this individual failed to turn up. Worse, the gas was far from pure, and his audiences suffered from headaches and sickness. But nothing discouraged Winsor. He improved his apparatus and made still more dazzling the prospect which he was offering to Britain.

How he managed technically is not clear. He must have possessed a spark of genius. He had never studied chemistry and was so little of a mechanic that he could not even describe to a workman how the apparatus he wanted should be made. But he knew how to sell. One gas lamp, he said (and proved), would give as much light as eighteen of the oil lamps then in use. This was an inducement to people who had groped about the murky streets, using a link boy with a torch if they could afford his hire. Gas could also be used for lighthouses. It could be used as a cure for asthma and chest diseases. It encouraged plants to grow. It 'did away with the dire necessity of the most wretched profession among men, that of our degraded and pitiable chimney sweepers'. In other words Winsor was the first to advocate not only a smokeless zone but a smokeless land. But his strongest argument was financial. To the nation he promised a saving of £120,000,000 a year if all raw coal were reduced to coke and gas. On top of that there would be a profit of £290,000,000 from the sale of these commodities. The national debt would be paid off in no time. Individual citizens were invited to buy £50 shares in the National Heat and Light Company on the promise that each share would bring in £6,000 a year.

Winsor was not consciously lying. He sincerely believed in the truth of his promises. Thus his words were the more convincing. And to back them he gave public demonstrations which seemed almost miraculous to the man and woman in the street.

He asked permission of the Prince of Wales to celebrate the King's birthday on 4 June 1807 by lighting the street between Carlton House and St James's Park. *The Monthly Magazine* thus described the demonstration:

The works had been for some time in preparation, and

private trials had previously been made to prove the air tightness of the tubes of communication, which were of tinned iron with soldered joints, except at certain distances where they are otherwise cemented together for the convenience of removal. The diameter of the long pipe is $1\frac{1}{2}$ inches; it commences in two close iron carbonising furnaces in Mr Winsor's house in Pall Mall, one capable of containing and coking four pecks and the other two pecks of common pit or sea coal . . .

The inflammable gas, which is quite transparent or invisible, began to flow in the pipes soon after 8 o'clock, and a lamplighter, or person with a small wax taper (the evening being quite serene) appeared and lighted the gas issuing from each burner in succession: some time after, a very large burner or assemblage of small streams of gas were lighted on the top of the transparency . . .

The light produced by these gas lamps was clear, bright and colourless, and from the success of this considerable experiment in point of the number of lights, the distance and length of pipe, hopes may now be entertained that this long-talked of mode of lighting our streets may at length be realized. The Mall continued crowded with spectators until near twelve o'clock, and they seemed much amused and delighted by this novel exhibition.

Winsor began to gather a Society of influential backers. Money came in, and he spent it on further demonstrations, being now technically assisted by an able chemist named Clegg. He spent all the money he received from investors – and more besides – on his project, never on himself. In October he asked permission of the parish paving committee to place specimen lamp posts outside his house in Pall Mall. It is not clear whether this permission was ever specifically given, but Winsor erected thirteen three-jet lamp posts along the south side of Pall Mall. Later he increased this number. But permission had to be obtained each time the lamps were lighted, and men were hired to watch them in case of accident.

On the business side, the Society met at the Crown and Anchor tavern in the Strand and decided to apply to the Chancellor of the Exchequer for a Charter of Incorporation for the New Patriotic Imperial and National Light & Heat Company, as the concern now called itself. On receiving this application the Chancellor of the Exchequer passed it on to the Privy Council. The Privy Council passed it to the King. The King, after a moment of puzzled embarrassment, passed it to the Law Officers of the Crown. They ruled that no such charter could be made effective without an Act of Parliament, so the Committee was back where it started.

When the necessary Bill was presented in Parliament it was hotly opposed. Against it were the vested interests of the oil lamp companies and firms like Boulton & Watt, and such individuals as Lord Dundonald and William Murdoch. Against it too were those die-hards who refused to believe that any commercial organization could benefit the country as a whole. But it is said that it was a facetious and witty speech of Wilberforce, the philanthropist, which caused the Bill's rejection.

It came back amended. On 9 June 1810 the Gas Light & Heat Company – the title, like the privileges requested, had been modified – was finally legally recognized. In 1814 permission was granted by the Vestry Committee of St James's parish to lay down gas mains in Pall Mall. In 1820 the whole parish was lit by gas.

In this hour of final triumph Winsor was in Paris, trying to get over another bankruptcy caused by the launching of a French company which aimed at lighting streets by gas. The London Society which he had formed, and which had evolved into the Committee of the Gas Light & Heat Company, had had no use for him. First a 'practical chymist' had been appointed in his place, leaving him only the vague duties of publicist and adviser. When he fled to France in 1815 to escape his English creditors the Committee removed his name from the board and stopped his annuity. He died in Paris in 1830. Through the initiative of his son, a memorial was erected to his memory in Kensal Green Cemetery with the inscription, 'At evening time it shall be light – Zach. xiv, 7.' His houses in Pall Mall were taken over by the Gas Light & Heat Company and by the Waterloo Museum, except for No. 93 which was occupied by a bookseller, R. H. Evans – a more cultural trend. But, according to the *Epicure's Almanack*, part of the Star and Garter building, 92, 'was degraded into a manufactory of shoe blacking'.

Thus we return to 1831 (nothing of interest having happened in the intervening decade) and to the Tory party in search of a headquarters. The Crown, as has been said, was always closely interested in buildings on its land, and the Commissioners of Woods and Forests, as the appropriate authority then called itself, was much in evidence early and late in the negotiations which followed.

At the end of 1833 demolition and subsequent building to the design of Sir Robert Smirke began on a ninety-foot Pall Mall frontage of the corner site described, and was completed in 1836. The Carlton, it will be remembered, was intended for a much more businesslike and specific purpose than any former club. It may claim some success in achieving this, for in 1842 the Tories were back in power with Peel at their head and Gladstone at his side. But by then the building had already proved too small. Long and difficult, even acrimonious, negotiations followed. After a ballot on the choice of architects' designs for enlargement westward, in which Sydney Smirke's firm came only fourth, he was chosen by the Club's Building Committee and was made responsible for the completed building, which involved refashioning the old.

Londoners, it seems, were no less critically conscious of new buildings then than now. Possibly they were more so. On the occasion of the Great Exhibition, when it might have been expected that architectural descriptions would for the sake of

15   Carlton House. The pillars and portico were later used for the National Gallery building

16   The National Gallery in Pall Mall. Sebastiano del Piombo's *Raising of Lazarus* is the biggest picture. Titian's *Bacchus and Ariadne* is on the right of the doorway. The crowded walls show the need for more space

foreign visitors be laudatory, the following assessment of the Carlton Club was published for the benefit of 'the stranger in our giant city':

The Carlton Club-house . . . exhibits in its present state a singular architectural antithesis, the addition made in 1847 by Sydney Smirke being utterly dissimilar in style and taste to the original structure erected by his brother, Sir Robert. Extremes certainly meet there, for we find what may be called the ultra-Italian in juxtaposition with that sort of Anglo-Greek which, after a short-lived vogue, has fallen into discredit; a taste for the florid having now superseded that for the frigid and the bald, which last passed in its day for the classical and the chaste. The new portion is little more than a direct and undisguised copy of Sansovino's Library of St Mark at Venice – a work whose celebrity converts into admiration the censure that this imitation of it would, were it an original composition, else incur for the monstrousness of its proportions, and violation of all orthodoxy and rule: nothing less than monstrous, in fact, can the entablature of the Ionic or upper order be pronounced, if it be tested by ordinary rules, more especially as it is considerably more ponderous than that of the Doric order below . . .

And so on with more phrases of severe and sonorous criticism. The only thing that this anonymous author came near to approving (except in its 'juxtaposition') was the use of red Peterhead granite for the shafts of the columns.

The rest of the façade was of Caen stone. A correspondent writing to *The Builder* in October 1847 said: 'If it be difficult to reconcile the mind to the colour of the two stones, how much more difficult must it be to do so in respect of the introduction of the most durable (granite) in respect of the most perishable (Caen) that has ever been used in London, and which in the course of twenty years will be swept by the hand of time with the besom of destruction.' He was just about right. The Caen stone crumbled, causing an endless series of expensive patchings-

up, until, to the designs of Sir Reginald Blomfield, the who
façade was renewed in 1923–24.

On the evening of 14 October 1940 the Carlton Club w
moderately full, Harold Macmillan, Lord Hailsham, and oth
now senior members of the Party being of the company. One
the usual air raids was in progress, and nobody was taking a
more notice than usual. A five-hundred pound high explosi
bomb fell on the club. But it struck a granite block. Against tl
'most durable stone' it exploded on impact instead of plungir
through to a lower floor. The building was wrecked beyor
repair, but no single person in it was even hurt.

The Carlton Club removed to 69/70 St James's Street, tl
former Arthur's Club-house. The ruin of the old building
Pall Mall, between the R.A.C. and Carlton Gardens, w
pulled down, and a handsome, severe, essentially modern ty;
of building erected in its place. At present it has no name ar
calls itself, with no apparent justification, No. 100 Pall Ma
It houses Lloyds Bank Europe, and the British Aircr
Corporation.

I

The Street of Palaces, 1851

I

IN 1851, THE YEAR of the Great Exhibition, a book of nearly a thousand pages, *London Exhibited,* edited from the contributions of anonymous authors by John Weale, was published for the benefit of visitors. Its description of club life at that time and as then remembered is interesting as such and incidentally as an expression of the Victorian point of view, aptly hall-marked with smugness. That was the era when the British male was really sure of himself – in Pall Mall at least.

As at present constituted, the London clubs and club life have produced a new phase in English society, at least in the metropolis – one which will claim the notice of some future Macaulay as showing the very 'form and pressure of the time'; which to the more patient chronicler of anecdotes, club-house traditions and reminiscences will afford material all the more interesting, perhaps, for not being encumbered with the dignity of formal history . . .

Until about thirty years ago a club was seldom more than a mere knot of acquaintances who met together of an evening at stated times in a room engaged for that purpose at a tavern, and some of them held their meetings at considerable intervals apart . . . The celebrated Literary Club which was founded by Reynolds in 1763 . . . consisted at first of only nine members, which number was however gradually increased to the large number of thirty-five; yet limited as it was it would not be easy even now to bring together as large a number of distinguished characters. The club dined together once a fortnight, on which occasion 'the feast of reason and the flow of soul' were no doubt enjoyed in perfection. In most clubs of that period, on the contrary, the flow of wine or other liquor was far more abundant than that of mind . . . It deserves to be remarked that though the older clubs encouraged compotation and habits of free indulgence as indispensable from good fellowship and sociability, the modern clubs on the contrary have done much to discourage them as low and ungentlemanly. 'Reeling home from a club' used to be formerly a common expression; whereas now insobriety, or the symptom of it, in a club-house would bring down disgrace on him who should be guilty of such an indiscretion . . .

From such meetings held periodically, they (the clubs) have become permanent establishments, luxurious in all their appointments; and of some of them the *locales* are quite palatial. No longer limited to a few acquaintances familiarly known to each other, they count their numbers in hundreds and, sleeping accommodation excepted, provide for them abundantly all the *agrémens* of an aristocratic house and admirably regulated *ménage,* without any of the trouble inseparable from a private household . . . In fact a modern London club is a realization of the Utopian *coenobium* – a sort of lay convent rivalling the celebrated Abbey of Theleme with its agreeable rule of *Fais ce que voudras* instead of a monastic discipline and mortification. Even a sybarite might be content with the studied and refined comfort which pervades every department of a West End club-house, and which is such as to be unattainable in a private family, except by the opulent.

The author lists the amenities of a club – news-room, coffee-room, library, writing-room, evening or drawing-room, card-room, billiard and smoking rooms. He lingers in the dining-room, becoming quite lyrical about the food.

Although it does not bear the words inscribed upon it, the *carte* seems to say FARE WELL, not as a phrase of dismissal but of welcome and invitation, its contents being such as to adapt themselves to the humour of every palate, since they range from roast beef and other joints *au naturel* to the most *recherché* sophistications of edible substances . . . To live upon the same scale and footing, to be surrounded by the same atmosphere of luxuriousness and refinement elsewhere, at anything like the same cost, is utterly impracticable . . . Club-house statistics would warrant our concluding that the average a head for wine and liqueurs is less than two shillings. The next point dealt with is management.

At the head of affairs is the Committee of Management, who are appointed from among the members and hold office for a certain time . . . They superintend all matters of expenditure and accounts . . . The Committee further appoint the several officers and servants, also the several tradespeople. The full complement of a club-house establishment consists of secretary and librarian, steward and housekeeper; to these principals succeed hall porters, groom of the chambers, butler, under-butler; then in the kitchen department clerk of the kitchen, *chef*, cooks, kitchen maids, etc.; lastly attendants, or footmen, and female servants . . .

The regularity which pervades the domestic economy generally is particularly remarkable in the kitchen department, for instead of anything like bustle, or that fuss which notable housewives seem to think essential to good management, all the culinary arrangements, multifarious as they are, are conducted with activity and dispatch, at the same time in the most orderly and methodical manner, towards which the arrangements of the place constitute not a little. In the Reform, and some of the other club-houses, the kitchen, with its manifold apparatus, machinery, and *modi operandi*, constitutes a perfect laboratory for scientific preparations of the most appetite-enticing kind.

All this, of course, is for men alone: women may only enter
club as junior servants. This is so obvious a law of life that o
author does not mention it. His following sentences are
interesting sociologically as architecturally.

The basement of a club-house requires quite as much
more study and contrivance than any other part of the pla
and in order to double the space to which it would else
confined, it is usually sunk to a good depth, so as to conta
an additional floor within it, that is, an entresol between t
lowermost or kitchen floor and the apparent external grou
floor. This economy of plan – which may be said to
particularly English – provides a complete habitation for t
domestic and official part of the establishment, and
invisible one also, provided it is properly screened out
dwarf parapet walls or balustrading, to prevent the area fr
being overlooked, as is done at the Travellers' and Refor
where such enclosure below enhances not a little the gene
effect of the elevation by producing a suitable architectu
base, and substituting the ornamental for the unsightly.
those club-houses which have baths, they and the dressi
rooms annexed to them are placed in the entresol . . .

The two chief apartments on the ground floor are t
morning-room and coffee-room, the first of which is the pla
of general rendezvous in the early part of the day, and
reading the newspapers. They are, of course, very spaci
apartments, though of comparatively sober character
though for the new Carlton coffee-room a high degree
ornateness has been studied. The only other room on t
floor is the House-Dining room, though it can hardly
reckoned among these, at least not among the 'show' roo
it being, it would seem, etiquette that it should be of extre
plainness, however lavishly other parts of the interior may
decorated. With regard to its peculiar denomination a
purpose it may be proper here to explain that although t
habitués of the club take their meals in the coffee-room, so

of the members occasionally – perhaps about once a month – make up a set dinner . . . and such *quasi*-private reunions around the 'mahogany' . . . are in club parlance styled house-dinners. Another room – which however is wanting in some club-houses – is an outer-room or waiting-room where a stranger can have an interview with a member.

Ascending to the upper or principal floor, we there find the evening or drawing-room, and card-room, the library and writing-room; the first mentioned of which is made the superlative degree, if not always of architectural effect, of the embellishment aimed at. With regard to the card-room, *Honi soit qui mal y pense!* – gambling and games of chance are interdicted; not even so much as what Lady Townley calls 'poor, piddling five-guinea whist' is permitted . . . The writing-room is also a very great accommodation for many gentlemen write their letters, and date from, their club . . .

The next or uppermost floor, which however does not show itself externally, it being concealed within the roof, is appropriated partly to the billiards and smoking-rooms . . .

Having explained the present club system, and the usual arrangement of a club-house, we shall now speak of the external character of the buildings of the kind, as features formerly quite unknown in our street architecture. Upon Pall Mall and its immediate vicinity – the former more especially – they have bestowed a certain nobleness of physiognomy of which no other part of the town affords an example, they being marked by a certain unmistakable quality as well as character, both of which distinguish them from all other buildings whether public or private. They may be said to be the only structures in the British capital that answer to the *palazzi* of the Italian cities.

II

ıE CLUBS which were the basis of the description of 1851 st concluded are, with the exception of the Carlton and the

Guards', still in Pall Mall. How they have changed in character will be discussed in a later chapter. Structurally they were almost exactly the same then as now, except for the addition of bedrooms.

It is somewhat artificial to list clubs according to age, for they were all founded in an adventitious meeting-place and were located for varying periods in temporary quarters before they found their site and put down permanent roots. So they will be described in the order in which they stand from east to west along Pall Mall. But the United Service and the Athenaeum were by any calculation in the first eleven of London clubs.

Before the end of the Napoleonic wars the fighting services had no club, apart from the Guards', which was of course restricted to the Brigade. Plans for a military club were hatched shortly before the Battle of Waterloo, when eighty senior officers assembled at the Thatched House Tavern in St James's Street on the invitation of Lieutenant-General Lord Lynedoch. This gallant old soldier has been mentioned before as Graham of Balgowan, the widower of the Hon. Mrs Graham who sat for Gainsborough.

The officers approved the plan. The Duke of Wellington endorsed it. And although the Prime Minister strongly disapproved of the army thus banding together in peace-time (he saw it in the light of the political clubs as a military junta), Lynedoch collected £10,000 and nearly 500 future members within four months. The Navy became associated, and the United Service waited in Albemarle Street for the site of a permanent clubhouse.

It will be clear from this procedure of starting with the collection of capital from future members that clubs by this time differed in organization from former clubs – with the exception of Arthur's (from 1811), the Union and the Guards' – in being members' clubs as opposed to proprietary clubs. The early clubs such as Boodle's and Brooks's were owned by the gentlemen who launched them. Such proprietors, whether individuals or small business groups, could take decisions over the heads of the members. But members' clubs are owned and run by the members themselves.

The idea of the Athenaeum – the Society as it was first called – 'for scientific, and literary men and artists' was born in the mind of John Wilson Croker. This was a first-class mind which had enabled Croker at the age of twelve to translate the first *Eclogue* and the first book of the *Aeneid* of Virgil into verse founded on the model of Pope's translation of Homer which he had learned by heart. In 1823, at the age of 43, he wrote to Sir Humphrey Davy, President of the Royal Society, saying that 'the fashionable and military clubs not only absorb a great proportion of society, but have spoiled all the coffee houses and taverns so that the artist, or mere literary man, neither of whom are members of the established clubs, are in a much worse position than they were.'

Having won the approval of the great scientist Davy, and a promise from the scarcely less distinguished, though younger, Michael Faraday, to act as temporary secretary, Croker set about forming a committee which included Sir Thomas Lawrence, President of the Royal Academy (who drew the head of Athene as the club seal), Sir Walter Scott, Samuel Rogers, the poet and art connoisseur whose art collection was sold at Christie's for £50,000, Sir Frances Chantrey, the sculptor, Joseph Jekyll, the barrister and wit, and of mere peers, Palmerston, Spencer, and Aberdeen.

From the first – and the club has ever since maintained this rule – Croker aimed high in the quality of membership. To artists (by his definition exhibitors at the Royal Academy) and to the authors of worthy books he added patrons of the arts, also bishops and judges 'who are *par etat* literary men although they may not have published any literary works.' Scientists, and professors in general, were eligible on their merits: they are in any case the most tireless writers of books, however limited their public. Notables – such people as kings, great statesmen, and ambassadors – were also admissible under a special rule. And it was much the same militarily in the building opposite. The result is that, looking at the list of members for the first or any year, one is reminded of Don Alhambra's song in *The Gondoliers,* with hardly a word needing to be changed to make it fit:

> Ambassadors cropped up like hay,
> Prime Ministers and such as they
> Grew like asparagus in May,
> Professors three a penny . . .
> Lord Chancellors were cheap as sprats
> And Bishops in their shovel hats
> Were plentiful as tabby cats –

But not, in point of fact, so many as is generally believed. At the time of writing there are not more than two-and-a-half dozen, far fewer than professors. While on the other side of Wellington Place

> On every side Field-Marshals gleamed,
> Small beer Lieutenant-Colonels seemed,
> With Admirals the armchairs teemed –

in the United Service.

Thus the ranks of valour and brains were organized, the United Service of about 1,500 men, the Athenaeum at that time restricted to 500, waiting only for permanent clubhouses. When in 1826 it was known that as part of the Regent Street development plan the house which had officially inspired it and on which the Regent had spent so much was, paradoxically, to be pulled down, the two Committees saw two ideal sites. These were on the corners of the south side of Pall Mall and the east and west sides of the future Waterloo Place. Within a few months of each other the Committees applied for the one of their choice; and when this much was granted the contest between Mars and Athene began. For its champion the United Service chose the most eminent architect of the day, while the Athenaeum chose one almost as young as David when he faced Goliath.

But it proved a three-cornered affair – or with even more awkward corners than a triangle. The chosen sites were key sites on Crown land, and never has the Crown taken a closer interest in proposed buildings. Clearly these had to be uniform, at least to the extent that they did not jar with each other. But the position was made anomalous by the fact that the architect commissioned by the United Service, John Nash, was also the chief architect of the Commissioners of Woods, Forests, and Land Revenues, while the architect of the Athenaeum was Decimus Burton, aged 24, who had not this advantage of being able officially to approve his own plans.

From the first the two clubs loved each other like brother and sister, and quarrelled as such, with the Commissioners acting the part of all-powerful but not entirely impartial parent. The to-and-fro of arguments, letters and plans is recorded clearly and in detail in that invariably excellent work, the *Survey of London*. Here one need only record that the disputes were amicably settled and the clubs admirably built, the United Service opening its doors to members on 18 November 1828 and the Athenaeum on 8 February 1830. The expenditure on the two buildings was as close as their opening dates: the United Service cost £43,700, the Athenaeum £43,101.

The only visible relic of their rivalry is the facsimile of the frieze of the Parthenon, added to the Athenaeum at the last moment, probably on the suggestion of W. R. Hamilton who had superintended the removal to England of the Elgin Marbles and was a member of the building committee. That, and the statue of Athene, compensated for any advantages held by the devotees of the God of War and their Crown Commissioners' architect. On the other hand nothing can conceal the particular interest of the site of the United Service, which was that of the early Royal Academy. As for membership, the Duke of Wellington belonged to both.

An interesting sequel to the architectural rivalry of the two clubs is that, after the death of Nash, the architect of the

Athenaeum became consultant architect of the United Service. Decimus Burton made considerable interior alterations and added to the club the building which adjoined it to the eastward. Twentieth-century alterations included the addition of squash courts and bedrooms, which cost about twice as much as the original building of the club.

Domestically, the club was at first stiff with service protocol. As army members only majors and above were eligible, and nothing less than a commander from the navy. But this rule dissolved when the Junior United Service was invited to amalgamate. This was effected in February, 1953, the junior club-house in Charles II Street being demolished to rise again as the home of the Atomic Energy Authority.

The domestic life of the Athenaeum is most appropriately left inside its handsome doors. The present author's strongest emotion on passing through them was a desire to slide down those ideally designed banisters. But whether this is forbidden under the rules was not put to the test. The reader must run for some of the excellent stories about the Athenaeum to a book specifically on clubs, those by Humphrey Ward, Bernard Darwin or Charles Graves, for instance. But it is not out of place to mention here that the only complaint about the new club-house was that it was stuffy. Long after gas lighting was invented, oil lamps were used in the coffee room on the insistence of the members.

The next building to the westward is the Travellers', which took its place in Pall Mall shortly after the completion of the Athenaeum. The club had already been in existence for a dozen years.

It was on 5 May 1819 that the first Committee decided 'to make Arrangements for the proposed Club'. The brevity of this statement matches the present-day reputation of the Travellers' for taciturnity: the members prefer reading to talking to each other, even at meals, though a guest may justly protest that he has been very adequately entertained there. This at least conforms with the originally stated purpose of the club – 'to form a point of re-union for gentlemen who had travelled abroad; and to afford them the opportunity for inviting, as Honorary Visitors, the principal members of all the foreign missions, and travellers of distinction', as the editor of *London Exhibited* put it in an earlier publication. Incidentally, 'travellers' were those who had ventured at least five hundred miles from England.

Among the distinguished Committee one finds the Lords Aberdeen and Palmerston again, and also W. R. Hamilton of the Elgin Marbles and Athenaeum frieze connexion. As early as that in the history of existing clubs it was the fashion to be a member of more than one, even within a few yards of each other – a step forward from the chauvinism of the political coffee-house derivation.

Starting in Waterloo Place, then moving to the site of Almack's Tavern and Brooks's first home, the Travellers' saw their chance to stop travelling when Carlton House was scheduled for demolition. (George IV might be the patron saint of the three clubs so far mentioned in this chapter: it is his only chance of sainthood.) The sites of four buildings to the west of the Athenaeum, 105–108, were vacant. The Travellers' who needed the space of three buildings, chose 105–107, leaving one between them and their future neighbour. Then the building committee instituted the first architectural competition for a club-house. (That for the Carlton Club building, though mentioned earlier here, was later in date.) Several architects, Decimus Burton among them, declined to compete. Among a second batch of invitations was Charles Barry, who was chosen.

The layman must always wonder at the patience of architects who produce so many highly finished drawings (some of them, after all, good enough artistically to hang in the Royal Academy), while comparatively few of them are translated into buildings. In this instance, leaving aside the unsuccessful competitors, Barry had to go back to his drawing-board again and again. Over four months after his plans had been accepted the Commissioners wrote to say that No. 105 Pall Mall could not be made available, but that the club could have 106–108 instead. This meant a considerable reduction in frontage. So completely new plans had to be drawn.

Then there was trouble with the Athenaeum, which wanted the Travellers' building to conform with its own. There was further trouble with the Commissioners, who had the last word, but finally permitted Barry a modicum of freedom from conformity. The building was completed by July 1832 for a little over £23,000, with a further £6,000 for furniture and fittings.

Charles Barry was well rewarded for his patient trouble, not only by his fee but by the favourable reaction which his building evoked. The judgement of 1851 was:

A structure that fairly makes an epoch in the architectural history of club-houses, as being almost the first, if not the very first, attempt to introduce into this country the species of rich *astylar* composition which has obtained the name of the Italian *palazzo* mode, by way of contradiction from Palladianism and its orders. Grecianism, Nashism, and Smirkeism had been exhausted, when, in an auspicious hour, both for himself and for the architectural design, Charles Barry seized upon a style that had been all along quite overlooked by English architects. What had till then been kept out of sight from the general public was hailed, not only as a pleasant novelty after the previous season of architectural dullness and insipidity, but received as originality also, though in fact there is very little of the latter in the façade towards Pall Mall, far less, indeed than in the design of the garden-front, which is not only greatly superior to the other, but shows a happiness of invention which the architect has certainly not surpassed, if approached, in his later works. That production of Mr Barry's may be said to have given a fresh impulse to architectural design, and one in a more artistic direction. It almost at once brought the style then adopted by him into vogue.

More than a hundred years later the opinion of architectural authorities has varied little, as the following quotation from the *Survey of London* shows:

The Travellers' Club is the first of Sir Charles Barry's masterpieces, a remarkably mature and brilliant work for a man of only thirty-four years, and one which exhibits most of his virtues and few of his faults. It may be that his refusal to conform with the stringcourses and cornice lines of the Athenaeum, already established by Burton, was a blow to the rule of uniformity in street architecture, but Rome, Florence, Venice and Genoa offered good precedent for Barry's non-conformity. His was the initial step taken in transforming Pall Mall into a *strada di palazzi,* variously echoing, with increasingly Victorian overtones, the masterpieces of Renaissance Italy.

The first of many interesting points about the Reform Club is the site on which it is built. In 1836 it began its Pall Mall life in No. 104, a Palladian-fronted building which for the five previous years had housed the King's pictures. This was demolished when the present club-house was decided upon, for it was to extend over the intervening houses to include the site of No. 100, the first home of the National Gallery.

A different aspect of the club's inauguration was that it derived from a union of the Whigs and Radicals, the latter being the more active launchers. But the first few years of club life saw the end of the Radicals as an effective parliamentary force. The reader may wonder whether this was purely coincidental or if the spikier forms of politics are incompatible with the smooth and gentlemanly associations of club life. The parliamentary unity of the club evolved into liberalism – a difficult word to define – and, specifically, support of the Reform Act of 1832. Once more we find the name of Lord Palmerston in the first list. Gladstone and Lord John Russell were also members, and in the present century Lloyd George, and Churchill in his liberal youth. But now politics have faded from the palatial scene and members are drawn from all parties except the Communist.

The building committee required that the club-house should 'surpass all others in size and magnificence'. In the architectural competition which they instituted both Barry and Burton were invited to compete, but Burton declined, so we cannot know which of the pair would have won. From the remainder, which included Sydney Smirke and Cockerell, Barry was chosen. He was therefore faced with the interesting task of surpassing his own masterpiece next door. The first plans having been passed in January 1839, the club-house was ready for occupation on 1 March 1841. Incvitably the building was expensive. The committee had stipulated to the competing architects that their estimates must not exceed £37,500. Following a request by all the competitors this was raised to £44,000. The final cost of Barry's building was in the region of £82,000, nearly the cost of the United Service and Athenaeum combined. The now familiar multiplication of the original estimate was in this case largely due to the elaborate fittings and sumptuous decorative work. Consequently it is the interior which is most striking to the average visitor. The first design had provided for an open court in the middle. On the suggestion of the building committee this was covered at roof level, creating on the ground floor an imposing hall, called the saloon, its great size seemingly increased by an enormous mirror, and on the first floor a wide gallery which gave access to all the principal rooms. It was this spaciousness which provided scope for decoration.

Curiously, our critic of 1851 made no mention of this striking feature. Of the interior he said only, 'In one respect this club-house differs from all the others, for whereas their elevations show only a ground floor and another over it, the Reform exhibits an additional upper storey, which is appropriated exclusively to sets of chambers or lodgings for such members as may engage them, which extra accommodation is quite peculiar to the club.' It was indeed. Most of the other clubs did

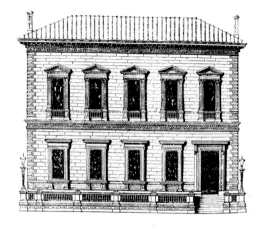

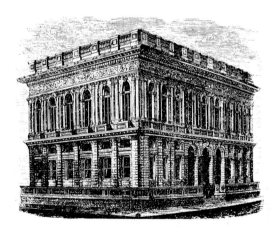

17 The Athenaeum,
Travellers', and
Army and Navy
Clubs in 1851

18   Looking eastward: the Reform, Travellers', Athenaeum, and United Service Clubs with Nelson's Column and St Martin-in-the-Fields on the horizon

not provide bedrooms until much later.

With regard to the exterior of the building he remarked: 'Of the three club-houses forming the *insula* or block of buildings on the west side of Carlton Place (Waterloo Place) the Reform is, though the latest, not the least', and then indignantly refuted the current gossip that it was a copy of the Palazzo Farnese in Rome, the work of Michelangelo and Sangallo. 'The only resemblance between the two structures consists in both of them being astylar, with columnar-decorated fenestration, while in all other respects the difference between them is so strong as to put likeness entirely out of the question. The blunder itself – for it can be called nothing else – would be hardly worth noticing, did it not show what inane and random stuff may be uttered with impunity, and pass uncontradicted on the subject of architecture.'

This contradiction did not put an end to the comparison. Barry's son, in his biography of his father, suggested that he had based his design of the Reform on that of the exterior of the Farnese. The *Survey of London* says with studied moderation: 'Comparison of the two buildings will soon show that the resemblance is superficial.' To the non-architect it seems that one could scarcely have a street described as a *strada di palazzi* without at least one of its buildings being compared with an actual *palazzo*.

Architecture apart, any account of the Reform would be sadly unbalanced without an appreciation of the genius who did more than anyone else – far more than Lord Palmerston, for instance – to make the young club famous. Politically its appeal was, by the very nature of democratic government, limited. But something was added to it which surpassed theories of government – outstandingly well-cooked food. All men are fundamentally greedy. It had at last become the fashion in England to believe that roast beef is not the only gastronomic gift of God. Those sufficiently well off in money and taste imported French cooks as they did Empire furniture.

Alexis Soyer, an adventurer, was not imported. At the age of 21 he came to England of his own accord to try his fortune. He was far from the conventional picture of a *chef*. He was an artist. He had wanted to be an actor. This early ambition was sublimated in eccentric dress and behaviour, in the compulsive wish to please and to be praised. This much was froth – the vain *poseur* with his floppy hat on the side of his head, the appearance and the apparent irresponsibility of Montmartre. Beneath it was a mathematically minded organiser and a brilliant creator.

In England he could choose his employer among rich *gourmets*. He served the Duke of Sutherland, the Marquis of Waterford, Sir Watkin William Wynn, the Marquess of Ailsa. But his ambitious spirit was not satisfied. He joined the Reform because he was there offered the opportunity to design his own kitchen in concord with one of the greatest architects of the day. The result was comparable to the textbook layout of a head-quarters and field of battle, the commander-in-chief in the centre of operations, lesser cooks so placed as to produce certain types of food at exact times, all the requirements readily to hand.

Soyer's kitchens of the Reform are fully described in a rare and beautiful book entitled *London Interiors*. Unfortunately, the style is too florid to permit quotations without exciting ridicule, whereas what should be evoked is wonder at the precision of arrangements – the calm 'activity and despatch' referred to in *London Exhibited*. The picture, which is from *London Interiors*, shows game birds lying on the floor. I believe this was no more than an artist's concession to old English tradition. But both evident and accurate is the portrayal of calmness and assurance in all concerned. Soyer was no hot-tempered driver. He was gentle, jovial, infectiously enthusiastic. He may be compared to a benign, revered Old Master who had all the students in his studio working so closely to his will that it is difficult for the connoisseur to distinguish what was done by his hand from that which was created under his guidance.

Soyer produced banquets of an artistic splendour quite for-gotten in this age of vitamins and calories. He is said to have created a dish which cost a hundred guineas. At the same time he put himself beyond the criticism of the most socially responsible by going to Ireland during the Famine to organize field kitchens which dispensed thousands of gallons of nourishing soup at next to nothing. He went to the Crimea, made salt pork edible with pleasure, and won the praise of Florence Nighting-ale. He wrote poems and an opera, and dozens of letters to *The Times*. He put the Reform on the map, not by politics or architecture but by proving the value of the adage, 'Feed the brute'.

III

THE ATHENAEUM, the Travellers' and the Reform made a self-contained block which, as pointed out in 1851, was 'remarkable for being treated architecturally throughout, and finished up on all four sides.' The other club-houses then in Pall Mall stood out from their neighbouring houses rather than combined with them. Still going westwards, the next building to the Reform, just beyond the narrow new street, Carlton Gardens, was the Carlton Club, still in the unbalanced form which called forth the criticism quoted in Chapter 10. Opposite to it, and completed only in February 1851, was the Army and Navy Club. This was and is only partially in our street, standing on the western corner of the westerly and now unnamed entrance from Pall Mall to St James's Square. But the Army and Navy cannot here be ignored, for in its excellent tactical position it has always commanded a wide arc of the southern side of Pall Mall. Part of the site was occupied by a house built about 1673 which belonged to Moll Davies for twelve years. This sturdy building was not pulled down until 1847. Moll Davies had bought it for £1,800. It was sold to the Army and Navy Club for £19,500.

Two architectural competitions were held, in the first of

which there were sixty-nine entrants, but none of the big names in club building. The final winners were the firm of Parnell and Smith, and building started in 1849. Of the result *London Exhibited* remarked: 'The Army and Navy Club-house . . . makes a very ambitious display, apparently out of rivalry for the Carlton. In like manner as for that building, here also a design of Sansovino's has been made use of, though with considerable deviations from the original, little more of it, in fact, being retained than that of the lower part, or basement, which is, nevertheless, more exceptionable in many respects than it is tasteful.'

In several respects the Club had a difficult start. It was first projected in 1837, when a number of army officers returning from India found no place for themselves in the existing military clubs, so they proposed to form their own. But the Duke of Wellington refused his essential patronage unless the Navy and Marines were admitted on an equal footing. How then could it rival the United Service? It soon became more popular, largely because it admitted visitors, and convivial men returning from exile naturally wanted to entertain their friends. The Army and Navy now admits ladies as associate members. Starting comparatively late, it has shown a knack of leading fashion.

Continuing westward, there were in 1851, as now, no more clubs on the north side of Pall Mall. On the south side there were none before almost the western end. The buildings which preceded the RAC were still to pass through an important phase before being demolished to make a site for the club. Thus the next club to the Carlton was the Oxford and Cambridge, two hundred strolling paces away. This is a peaceful place, containing more churchmen than any other club except the Athenaeum. But it may be that the ghosts of Sir Robert Walpole and Sarah, Duchess of Marlborough, are still quarrelling about it. In the early eighteenth century the only access to Marlborough House was from Marlborough Gate, the short road between Pall Mall and the Mall. The Dowager Duchess wanted to make an entrance from Pall Mall through No. 71 and the houses behind it. Walpole, who disliked her intensely, wanted to prevent this, and being at the time First Lord of the Treasury was able to do so by getting control of Nos. 69–71. These houses remained until 1835, when No. 71 was knocked down for the building of the Oxford and Cambridge. Incidentally, the present set-back entrance to Marlborough House dates only from 1928.

The resolution to form the club was reached at a 'numerous Meeting of Members of the Universities of Oxford and Cambridge' in May 1830, over which Lord Palmerston presided. Building started at the end of 1835 and was completed at the beginning of 1838. The brothers Smirke were the architects, though Robert was mainly concerned. 'Smirkeism', as we know, was not the favourite school of the Great Exhibition critic, who briefly commented: 'The design betrays some conflict of opposite tastes. For the interior, economy seems to have been chiefly consulted; and appearance has been, somewhat unpardonably, altogether disregarded for the south side, although it should have been attended to there – because it is seen from the courtyard of Marlborough House.' A contemporary periodical, however, remarked that the building had 'an air of monumental grandeur, admirably suited to a building, which, from its connection with the Universities, awakes attention to those proud features of our Constitution.' And the *Survey of London* sums up: 'The design is certainly bold in scale by London standards; the style (Greco-Roman and Italianate) and the material (painted stucco) relate it to the great clubhouses in Waterloo Place, and a note of Regency elegance is sustained by the use of slender glazing-bars in the sash windows.' The first club committee appear to have accepted the plans almost exactly as first submitted. The only thing they argued about was whether or not there should be a smoking room. They took two meetings to decide in favour, and the voting was close.

The Guards' Club remains to be mentioned. It was on the site of No. 70 – one of the houses which had been in dispute between Sir Robert Walpole and Sarah, Duchess of Marlborough. The Guards' Club had been founded as early as 1813, being accommodated in St James's Street before coming to Pall Mall in 1849. There Henry Harrison built them the smallest club-house in the street, but one which gained the praise of the severe critic of 1851. He described it as 'remarkable for its compactness and convenience, although its size and external appearance indicate no more than a private house'. In 1920 the club moved to Brook Street for a while, and Barclays Bank, which lived next door, rebuilt both 69 and 70.

12

Burial of a Tradition

Great in council and great in war,
Foremost captain of his time,
Rich in saving common-sense,
And, as the greatest only are,
In simplicity sublime.

Lord Tennyson

ON THURSDAY 18 November 1852 Pall Mall formed part of
the route of a great and solemn procession. *The Times* said that
in a hundred years there might be 'some score of old people in
this country who will talk to incredulous hearers of the Duke of
Wellington's funeral'. Sir Winston Churchill's funeral, with
which the modern reader will naturally compare it, fell a dozen
years beyond the century. One wonders if anyone who was
present at the first as a small child was still alive to see the
second on television.

Churchill died nearly twenty years after VE Day, and it was
a few months less than that since he had last held office.
Wellington died thirty-seven years, more than a generation,
after the Battle of Waterloo. Since then he had been an old
soldier and an elder statesman, a clubman with simple, old-
fashioned English tastes in food and everything else, except
gambling. (His invariable club lunch was a cut off the joint, and
the horse-blocks between the United Service and Athenaeum
were put there for his convenience.) Above all else he was a
great and untarnished name. Marlborough, the victor of
Blenheim, Oudenarde and Malplaquet, but a much less
straightforward character, was much less popular. The number
of people who witnessed the procession which escorted Welling-

ton's body along the Mall, Constitution Hill, Piccadilly, St James's Street, Pall Mall, the Strand, Fleet Street and Ludgate Hill to St Paul's Cathedral was variously estimated, by *The Times* as 'near a million' and by other authorities as a million-and-a-half. Many of them had waited in the rain all night. The population of London at the time was less than two and a half millions.

Such a volume of public sympathy had not been expected. The first leader of *The Times* next morning is worth quoting at length. It starts with what appears lofty criticism but turns out to be surprise, which it explains away to itself and to its readers in the course of the article.

London yesterday must have fared ill in the sober judgement of a stranger unacquainted with the history and character of the British people. The whole population appeared bent upon feasting its eyes with a funeral pageant of no extraordinary beauty, the subject of which was a man whose death had long been a matter of constant expectation. The passion had assumed the form of a positive monomania . . . As the Chancellor of the Exchequer observed, an economical nation had rejected all thought of expense, a practical nation had surrendered itself to a mere sentiment, a busy nation had resolved to waste a day, an unostentatious nation had all of a sudden determined on a pompous display of public affliction. Not a single institution or arm of the state . . . but volunteered its part . . . So the principal thoroughfare for half the length of the metropolis was converted into a theatre of this great national eulogy . . . While it was yet dark the pavements were occupied and the barriers threatened with the impatient admirers of a man infinitely above the condition of the vulgar, and who never made much profession of sympathy for it. 'The city is mad' said a few cynical observers. But the country was mad too. Though floods had interrupted the railway traffic, and the barometer was below 'much rain'; though the day before had been showery, and the night promised still worse; though the streets were ankle deep in mud and the average accommodation was a guinea a sitting, still London was full of country folks attracted by the name of a man whose greatness in their minds was little more than a tradition from their fathers . . .

Now, whence is this madness?

There follows a long paragraph assessing the qualities and achievements necessary for the British to acclaim a man a hero, and the conclusion is reached that only once in several centuries does a country 'not particularly prone to idolize her great men' give way to wholehearted admiration. But that when this happens it is well justified.

This is not madness. It was an act of soberness and truth . . . We have long husbanded our admiration, and have now found a man entitled to it. Let the memory of that great man be cherished and honoured; for by him the Lord hath wrought our deliverance.

The Morning Post, its pages edged with black, is more conventionally laudatory. Its leading article begins: 'It is over. The "good grey head" lies low. The great name rises, as did the constant purpose of its glorious bearer, higher and yet higher.' But it picks up the interesting point about the relations of Wellington with the common people. Having enumerated the official bodies present at the funeral – 'There were – more than all these – swarming to see the last of their hero – the wayward, uncertain masses of the people, who are the children of the State – for whose good the Duke worked far more truly than ever did their self-styled special friends – the wayward, but, in the long run, well-judging people, who admired, feared, misunderstood, but at last loved and almost idolised the Duke.'

His body had lain in state in the Great Hall of the Royal Hospital at Chelsea where many of his old soldiers were Pensioners. There on 11 November, a week before the funeral, Queen Victoria, the royal family and members of foreign royal houses paid their respects. Next day entrance was by tickets, issued by the Lord Chamberlain to foreign Ambassadors, Peers, Members of Parliament and the like. On the 13th to 17th, Sunday the 14th excepted, the public were admitted. There is no record of how many filed past the coffin. It was constantly attended by detachments from the Brigade of Guards and the Lord Chamberlain's Department. We learn from the *London Gazette*'s special publication that these did not stand but sat at the head and sides of the coffin. But 'Warders of the Tower were stationed on the Dais, during the whole time of the Lying-in-State'.

On the 17th the coffin was removed to the Audience Chamber of the Horse Guards, preparatory to the funeral next day. On the 18th no troops lined the streets: this was left to the police; but a large military force led and closed the procession. This consisted of seventeen pieces of artillery, eight squadrons of cavalry and six battalions of infantry, including one of Marines, each of 640 rank and file – over 4,000 soldiers. There was of course a very large number of civilian followers as well who with their carriages occupied quite as much space. There were ten military bands which took over the solemn music from each other like so many echoes.

Before dawn on the 18th the troops mustered on the Horse Guards Parade under the command of Major-General the Duke of Cambridge, the civilians in St James's Park. *The Times* reported:

> The day broke heavily, the wind being loaded with moisture, the sky threatening-looking, and the streets giving a most unequivocal token of a night of heavy rain . . .
>
> At half-past 7 o'clock the coffin was removed from the chamber in which it had rested during the night and with the aid of machinery was raised to its position on the lofty summit of the car. At 8 o'clock the hangings of the tent which concealed it from view were suddenly furled up. The first minute gun was fired, upon which the roll of the muffled drum, followed by the music of the Dead March in *Saul*,

announced that the procession had commenced. This was certainly one of the most impressive and striking features of the ceremonial . . . The men, of course, carried their arms reversed, which, combined with the mournful music and the slow funeral pace at which they marched, had a singularly imposing effect. To the troops the mourning coaches and carriages, properly marshalled, succeeded; and the length of the procession may be imagined when we state that though the Rifles led the way at 8 o'clock it was 25 minutes past 9 o'clock before the car started, and half-an-hour later before the extreme rear was in motion. Let the reader who did not witness the spectacle endeavour to picture in imagination the stately pomp and military pageant passing in long column along the spacious avenue of the Mall, and then winding up Constitution-hill, while thousands upon thousands of spectators, in respectful silence, witness its progress . . .

The funeral car is described:

'The whole lower part is of bronze, supported on six wheels and elaborated with an amount of skill and artistic feeling which deserves unqualified praise. Above this metallic framework rises a rich pediment of gilding, in the panels of which the following list of victories is enstitched' – twenty-six in all, ending with Waterloo. On top of the coffin lay the Duke's hat and sword. The car was drawn by twelve enormous black horses 'completely covered with velvet housings, having the arms of the deceased splendidly embroidered on them . . .'

The funeral car was enormous – twenty-seven feet long, ten feet broad, seventeen feet high, and weighed over two tons. It came near to causing disaster. Of the moment when the head of the procession had reached the western end of Piccadilly the *Morning Post* reported: 'Great excitement and alarm was created by the Duke of Cambridge galloping in hot haste, followed by two aides-de-camp, through the archway (at Hyde

Park Corner) and ordering the procession to stop.'

The trouble was this. The funeral car had at that time only travelled a few hundred yards, for it was preceded by the majority of the military units, by a representative of every regiment of Her Majesty's Service, including the East India Company's army, by the College of Arms, the Standard, Guidon and Banners with those bearing them and those in support, by coaches carrying representatives of the Merchant Taylors' Company, the East India Company, Trinity House, the Cinque Ports, the Duke's Household, the Heralds, the Law, the Church, by Prince Albert, by the bearers of the Batons of the Armies of Spain, Russia, Prussia, Portugal, the Netherlands and Hanover, of a Field Marshal's Baton of the British Army and of the Duke's coronet, and by the eight Generals who were pall-bearers.

Running across the Mall below the line of Waterloo Place and Steps there was a gutter some inches deep. It had been filled with gravel and earth, but the rain had softened this. The wheels of the funeral car sank in it and stopped. The twelve black horses with their nodding plumes could not get the car started again. Policemen lining the roadway and civilian volunteers came forward in ones and two to help and then in greater numbers, while those so inclined shouted advice. But for a quarter of an hour the car remained stuck, the forepart of the procession continued on its way, and spectators from Pall Mall poured to the top of Waterloo Steps, and as far down them as they could force their way, to watch how the crisis would be resolved.

This is what they saw: around the mud-stuck car were Garter King-of-Arms and his attendants, and the senior officers on horseback who bore the Bannerols of the Lineage of the Deceased. Directly behind them were the Chief Mourner, the new Duke, in 'a long mourning cloak', and seventeen coaches of family mourners. Behind this black, impressive column stood patiently an old man with a horse, a pair of riding boots and spurs suspended from the saddle. These were John Mears, Wellington's groom, and his old charger. What, one wonders, were their thoughts.

At last the car was re-started and the procession continued on its way without any other awkward incident along Piccadilly and down St James's Street. Let the reporter of *The Times* take over:

The line of the procession now led along the region of the clubs, the fronts of which were for the most part filled up with balconies draped in black, and there, or within the shelter of wide plate-glass windows sat immense numbers of ladies provided with places by the courtesy and gallantry of the members . . . The car had reached the foot of St James's Street about half-past ten, having occupied an hour on its way there from the Horse Guards. It, therefore, became evident that it would arrive at the Cathedral in excellent time . . .

The great clubs along Pall-mall overflowed with visitors, and their handsome architectural proportions never looked more striking or beautiful than when thus animated and relieved by such vast assemblages of well-dressed people. The Oxford and Cambridge Club, the Army & Navy, the Carlton, the Reform, the Travellers' and the Athenaeum, all swarmed with occupants, their balconies being hung with black, and hosts of ladies appearing in the best seats. Perhaps along the whole route there was no single street which presented more objects of attraction and greater facilities for observation to foot passengers than Pall-mall . . . There was something particularly touching in the muster of old officers at the Senior United, many of whom looked with unusual earnestness at the great car, as with its illustrious burden, to the roll of drums and the fitful strains of martial music, it rolled upon its way.

The *Morning Post*'s reporter added further details:

There were few portions of the route which presented a

more picturesque and imposing appearance than the line of street extending from St James's Palace to Waterloo-place. For many days and nights previously the most strenuous exertions were made to provide accommodation for the more favoured portions of the public who had secured seats in the various club-houses and public establishments along the line. The private houses and shops had their balconies strengthened by means of timber supports, while in many instances stages were erected on the roofs and other prominent places from which a glimpse of the procession could be seen. At Marlborough House rows of seats were erected extending from the gate in Pall Mall back to the Chapel Royal. The front balconies of the Oxford and Cambridge Club were tastefully hung with black cloth, festooned with silver lace, the letter 'W' enclosed in laurel wreaths, being inserted in temporary hatchments. A covered gallery was raised even with the ground floor and provided with seats for some 200 or 300 persons. We observed that the Carlton Club had no visitors, and no public breakfast. This was in good taste. The Duke was the founder of the Carlton, and continued a member until the last hour of his life. We were glad, therefore, to see that tokens of mourning, and not indications of frivolity, were manifested at this aristocratic institution. The members of the Army and Navy Club, at the corner of George-street, St James's Square, availed themselves to the utmost of the extended frontage of their magnificent new building. In the reading-room, tiers of seats were raised at every window, and a gallery was erected around two sides of the building. The balconies of the windows of the upper floor were covered with black cloth, and seats were provided on the roof which commanded a splendid view of the line of the procession as far as Trafalgar Square. In front of the Ordnance-Office, but within the iron railings, seats were constructed for the accommodation of many hundred persons. Raised galleries were also erected in front of the Reform, the Travellers', and Athenaeum Clubs . . . At Schomberg House (Messrs. Harding & Co's) adjoining the Ordnance-Office, two spacious galleries were erected . . .

The United Service Club-house, which generally takes the initiative whenever any general spectacle of a national character takes place, was crowded with visitors . . . The funeral car was detained for rather more than five minutes when it arrived opposite the Athenaeum Club. The spectators here raised their hats while the car remained stationary, but the most profound stillness prevailed among the multitude . . . The procession was exactly two hours passing through Pall Mall. Some approximate idea of the numbers who witnessed the spectacle may be gathered from the fact that, at the lowest calculation, one hundred and twenty thousand persons were collected in Pall Mall alone.

At Charing Cross eighty-three Chelsea Pensioners joined the procession and marched with it along the Strand, down Fleet Street, and up Ludgate Hill to St Paul's Cathedral.

Royal recognition was conveyed in the following notice:

The Queen has been graciously pleased, through the Right Hon. Mr Secretary Walpole, to express Her Majesty's entire approbation of the arrangements made in the department of the Earl Marshal of England, on the memorable occasion of the Funeral of the late Field Marshal the Duke of Wellington, and commanded the Earl Marshal to communicate to the Officers who acted under his authority in carrying these arrangements into execution, the sense of their services which Her Majesty has been graciously pleased to express.

NORFOLK,
Earl Marshal.

19a Staircase and landing at the United Service Club

19b The hall of the Athenaeum

20   The Oxford and Cambridge Club

21 The saloon, first floor gallery, and the kitchen of the Reform Club

22   The Duke of Wellington's funeral procession

13
The Junior Carlton Club

CHARLES GRAVES tells a story about the Secretary of the Junior Carlton receiving a letter from a German Pen Club which began 'Dear Boys and Girls'.

The members of the Junior Carlton are not necessarily young. Although there is a minimum age limit, no maximum is stipulated. In fact, as far as the rules are concerned, its members might have witnessed the Duke of Wellington's funeral procession – from another building. Therein lies the significance of 'Junior'. The club was only founded in 1864 because a number of Tories were discouraged by the length of the waiting list for the Carlton. They created an even more active party hive, with a higher proportion of workers to drones. They form the most truly political club in London, and politics does not depend on age. But the club-house was built about equidistant in time between the palaces described in Chapter 11 and Pall Mall's great clubs of this century. It is betwixt and between.

The club-house was built by David Brandon in the High Victorian age and was aptly described in the *Survey of London* as a High Victorian echo of the Reform. It had, and still owns, a splendid site, just across George Street from the Army and Navy. George Street has recently had its name erased, to become no more than the short, anonymous connection with Pall Mall from the south-west corner of St James's Square.

Between this and the south-easterly connection there was formerly an undistinguished cluster of buildings. The Junior Carlton greatly improved the standard of this lot, and, matching well with the Army and Navy, made something well worth looking at on the north side. But one cannot help being sorry that no one took a piece of advice of 1851, given regretfully because – it being at the time not known that other clubs would be born – it was believed to be too late. This was that the whole *insula* between the south side of St James's Square and Pall Mall should be developed as a single block of clubs. 'The structures would have had the advantage of a double frontage either way of a most desirable kind. Although varied in design they would have formed a continuous range of stately façades, an *insula* similar to that of the west side of Carlton Place (Waterloo Place); besides which, St James's Square itself would have been most materially improved, for the houses which now occupy its south side rather disfigure its general appearance than not.'

The main part of the site acquired by the Junior Carlton was that of the house of Sir Hugh Pallister, previously mentioned as a neighbour of James Christie and a man who suffered from Courts Martial and the mob. In 1886 the club acquired the contiguous Adair House as an extension, and in 1925 No. 29, previously occupied for well over a hundred years by the Royal Exchange Assurance. This it turned into a ladies' annexe.

The Junior Carlton's club-house was a fine building, interestingly furnished. It contained among many other pieces of interest Disraeli's table which, without or with its extensions, can accommodate between twelve and seventy-four people. The house, with later building on to the roof, exceeded the official limit in height. For this it is at the time of writing doing penance by being a deep hole in the ground. Therefore one is discouraged from giving a fuller architectural description.

Since the first club was formed, this type of social life has been popular. It is difficult to picture London without clubs. They provide scope for the gregarious and a comfortable refuge for the recluse. They are all things to all men. What more can they offer? But they were born under a constellation which sees to it that even the most splendid is in constant anxiety about money.

Curiously, they were most stable in the first quarter of a century which followed the founding of the first subscription clubs – say 1765 to 1790. Ever since, although there were more and more potential members, and club secretaries presumably learned better and better how to order their affairs, there are few clubs which have not felt – or at least imagined that they felt – the cold breath of bankruptcy on the back of their necks. Club Committee minutes are largely concerned with reducing expenditure and increasing receipts. Many clubs have been driven to desperate measures such as waiving the entrance fee or admitting women. That was before the Fairy Godmothers came along. The modern Fairy Godmother waves a measuring rod, summoning up contemporary genies (which have the form of cranes, bulldozers and concrete mixers), and within a year or two the club has brand-new premises on the same site with quite as much accommodation as before – and nothing to pay.

Like all great inventions, this one is so simple that you wonder why nobody thought of it before. It depends on the principle that you own the air above your home, at least to the height at which aeroplanes fly. Therefore, the Westminster City Council permitting, any London house can be extended upwards to increase – perhaps double or treble – the accommodation on that site. The extra accommodation is let to pay for the old: the more expensive the site, the better the prospects. Actually, of course, the house is not made taller. It is demolished and a higher building constructed on the site. The Junior Carlton has submitted itself to this form of magic. (That is why it is at the moment a hole in the ground.) Its neighbour the Army and Navy did something different. It exchanged the freehold of its annexe for the construction of a new, larger and modern-to-the-minute building on the rest of its site. In this case the Fairy Godmother was Charles Clore. On the face of it both clubs are, or will be, better off – on the metaphorical face of it, that is. In the eyes of the conservatively minded the actual face of a club so treated is less handsome than before.

But at least the Junior Carlton will no longer be betwixt and between. It will be the very latest thing in Pall Mall, living up to its juniority.

14
W.D. - Mafeking - R.A.C.

It was a joke of the two World Wars that major strategy was settled in the armchairs of the clubs. The two Boer wars were in truth conducted from Pall Mall. The Ordnance Office, later to be called the War Office, was already installed next to Schomberg House, and in some other Pall Mall houses also, at the time of Wellington's funeral. Thereafter it increased the area of its invasion until it was occupying Nos. 80 to 91 inclusive. It remained in Pall Mall until after the turn of the century.

No attempt will be made to describe what it did there. Instead we will glance at the buildings which it occupied, some of which have already been mentioned. It is to the credit of the War Office that it only pulled down and rebuilt one house: the rest it merely occupied and, in time, vacated.

Nos. 80–82 was and is Schomberg House, that museum of human types with which we are not yet finished. The War Office used it as a single building for the first time since Beau Astley had divided it into three. The chairborne soldiers appear to have been happy there, for although the rest of the War Office moved to its great new building in Whitehall in 1906 the Director of Barrack Construction remained at Schomberg House. It was in fact retained for the use of government offices until 1936, thus completing a tenure of almost a hundred years. Another good mark to to the War Office is that, having more influence than a private individual, it was able to obtain from the Crown the relaxation of an order which had been made to pull down and rebuild Schomberg House in 1865.

Numbers 83–84 originally belonged to Lady Ranelagh. It

will be remembered from Chapter 2 that she owned and used two houses side by side. In the later part of the eighteenth century the lease passed to James Christie. In 1850 the two houses were pulled down and a single office building was constructed for the War Office.

The Duke of York (uncle of the grand old Duke who had ten thousand men and exercised them so futilely) bought Nos. 85–87 in 1760, and pulled them down to build York House on the site of 86. This was enlarged by the addition of 85 and 87, and called Cumberland House, when it passed to his brother. Thus one of the former tenants of the first War Office was Bloody Cumberland. Another, going back further, before Prince Charles Edward's defeat at Culloden, was the owner of the Cocoa Tree, the Jacobite stronghold. As in many of Pall Mall's houses one can imagine the ghosts not getting on together very well – ghosts haunted by older ghosts.

Number 88 had been occupied by the portrait painter, Nathaniel Hone, the best miniaturist of his day and one of the few enemies of Sir Joshua Reynolds. No. 89 had at the start of the century been a hatter's, with big bay shop windows, owned by the Wagner family before passing to the Globe Insurance Company. No. 90 was until 1849 the house of William Joseph Denison, probably the richest man who ever lived in Pall Mall. His father had come to London from Yorkshire as a youth and by sheer hard work made a fortune. William multiplied it several times by his successes as merchant and broker. He never married. He left £500 to charity and £1,800,000 to his nephew, Lord Albert Conyngham, on condition that he took the name of Denison only.

Number 91 was Buckingham House. The early history of this house as owned by the rising family of Grenville which became, via Earl and Marquess, Dukes of Buckingham and Chandos, has already been touched on. The later history is of a rapid decline. The first Duke made extensive improvements to the house, employing Sir John Soane as architect. He then became short of money and had to borrow from his architect. The Travellers' made an offer of £25,000 for the house, which he refused as being too low. But his son, Richard Plantagenet, had to sell for what he could get to pay off his debts. It was bought by a speculator named Kensington Lewis, who had the grandest ideas on what he would do with it. But the Crown was not much impressed by them because he did not pay his rent. Buckingham House was unsuccessfully put up for auction. The Junior United Service thought of buying it, and the Carlton used it while its own extension was in progress. In 1855 the War Office took it over.

Thus the War Office was installed along the south side of Pall Mall from Schomberg House to the walls of the Carlton Club – a stretch of one hundred and thirty yards. In 1856 it had been suggested that the War Department, which had just absorbed the Ordnance Office, should build a permanent headquarters in Pall Mall, as witness *The Builder* of 12 April in that year: 'It may be erected in Pall Mall on the site of Buckingham House and adjoining premises between that and the Ordnance Office'. The building would, it continued, 'be of a grand national character'. As such it was proposed to hold an international architectural competition so that the best possible plans should be obtained. The proposal to open the competition to foreign as well as British architects is a measure of the importance attached to the proposed building.

If this suggestion had been put into effect not only the appearance but the whole character of Pall Mall would have been changed, for one can easily imagine the ever-growing War Department snapping up one more building after another as they became available. How often some decision, soon forgotten, might have completely changed a scene we know. As it is, the War Office is forgotten in Pall Mall. Long before the Army became mechanized most of its buildings were taken over by the Royal Automobile Club. But before turning to that phase it seems appropriate – since Pall Mall has no reason to be anything but grateful to its guest – to mention one of the few occasions when the War Office went to bed happy.

The first Boer war of 1880–81 was outstandingly inglorious as far as Britain was concerned. The second, 1899–1902, started as badly. Before the end of October 1899 the British forces were hemmed in at Ladysmith, Kimberley and Mafeking. It is no part of this book to describe that unhappy war as a whole, but while writing this chapter I have by a strange coincidence come upon a diary of my father, who fought in South Africa. The start is worth quoting as showing that the War Office was accepting the course of events with remarkable calm.

While we were still trying to realize the full force of the news of that awful week (the disasters of Colenso, Magersfontein and Stormberg) an Army Order was issued by the War Office inviting members of the Yeomanry Regiments to volunteer for active service in South Africa. Earlier in the autumn several Yeomanry Corps had offered to send out men, but their offer had not been accepted at the time. Now, however, their chance had come, and many were eager to make the most of it.

In the papers of December 20 there appeared a copy of this Army Order, and that same day I and many others sent in applications to the War Office volunteering our services. It was not, however, till after Christmas that we received any answer. At first the War Office authorities in Edinburgh replied that they had received no instructions. But during Christmas week we received orders to report . . .

There were only a few of us who attended at the War Office that first morning, but they were a very representative sample . . . an old Scots Greys trooper, a solicitor, an English barrister, a medical student, a corn merchant from Syria, and a boy who had just left school. The ordeal of inspection before the Recruiting Medical Officer, which followed, was a most trying one, but the relief of being passed fit made up in great part for the cold and discomfort.

The shooting trials were held one bitter cold morning with the snow lying thick on the ground and a dark shadow veiling the targets. Then followed the riding tests and after that a week of further suspense.

On January 7 came news that we were to attend at the Riding School to be sworn in. The required numbers were now complete – thirty Yeomen and about eighty civilians.

So much for the state of mind at home. In South Africa – to take just one example – Mafeking had been invested on 15 October. It was a straggling and very isolated town in the north of Cape Province which had grown up as a centre of communications. As such it was strategically important, but it was not by nature easy to defend. The commander of the small military force was Colonel Baden-Powell, whose Chief of Staff was Major Lord Edward Cecil. At the start of hostilities Colonel Baden-Powell mobilized the male civilians. One woman, Lady Sarah Wilson, left Mafeking on the night of the day when war was declared and was thereafter instrumental in getting dispatches out of the town. So something at least about the progress of the siege was known in England.

At the beginning of May 1900, when Mafeking had been besieged for six and a half months, it was known in London that the relief force must be close to the town. The heroic defence had fired the imagination of all in England and news was awaited daily, even hourly.

Let us turn to the newspapers. The *Pall Mall Gazette* of Saturday 19 May described the scene in Fleet Street the evening before:

It was seventeen minutes past nine o'clock when the message containing the official announcement from Pretoria (the *enemy* capital) that the Boers had abandoned the siege, and that a British force, advancing from the south, had taken possession of the garrison began to come over the tape from Reuter's Agency. *The Daily Telegraph* had the felicity of being the first to convey the intelligence to the public by means of a placard in the front window of their office . . . Strangers shook one another by the hand; staid folk forgot their staidness; the infection of the cheering spread like wildfire, and the news was carried through the streets of London like a flash.

The reporter of the *St James's Gazette* was at that time in the Strand.

The streets were comparatively empty. The last carriage had delivered its burden at the theatre or the opera, and the last workman had got away to his suburban home . . . The people who walked the Strand were for the most part merely killing time, deluding themselves that they were enjoying fresh air – fancy, fresh air in the Strand! – after work . . .

Ten o'clock had just struck when a restless movement among the crowd who made their way eastward attracted our attention. The first isolated cheers rose above the noise of the traffic until, gathering strength and body, they swelled into a mighty roar that drowned all else. The paper carts dashed up showing tri-coloured bills, the newsvendors pounced upon them, fastening upon the papers, tearing these away, and setting off at a run in various directions. Numberless flags had sprung up, to every third person a flag, while a few, more patriotic or lavish than the rest of us, carried two.

As the buses met they greeted each other, waving hats and sticks. The cabmen tied small flags to their whips, and used them for portable flagstaffs. Nobody made any comment; it was too early for that; they simply cheered in a hoarse, gruff, discordant manner, but the cheering came from the heart. Nobody even asked particulars; for a short time few people even enquired what was the source of information. It was enough to know that Mafeking was relieved, the morning would bring the rest . . .

Streams of people poured into Pall Mall from every side, cautious, sceptical people who wished to read for themselves, who would not be satisfied until they found the news for themselves. And for them there was disappointment.

NO NEWS

The square card hung on the pillar of the central door of the War Office, drooping a little sideways, as if wishing to apologise for its unwelcome reserve.

The Pall Mall Gazette:

By eleven o'clock Pall Mall was full of people, the stationary throng in front of the War Office being provided with two mobile wings, each including a number of processions marching backwards and forwards, with all kinds of patriotic demonstrations. There must have been 30,000 persons in the street and they showed not the slightest desire to go home.

The wild celebrations, the 'maficking', to use a word which was coined from that night, continued until the small hours when the porters at Covent Garden took it up. 'London is still cheering', wrote a weary reporter for the last edition, 'and it does not seem that it will ever stop'. It did not stop for at least another twenty-four hours. And in all this time there was still NO NEWS as far as the War Office was concerned, for nothing had come through the proper channels. But that made no difference – except that the Government Offices flew no flags.

The Manchester Guardian's London correspondent described Saturday:

Men, women and children stepped briskly out of the morning trains carrying Union Jacks instead of the usual umbrellas ... Most of the innumerable processions of the day marched, or rather danced, along under the inspiration of this hackneyed melody (*Soldiers of the Queen*). People, indeed, showed no sign of ever getting tired of hearing the same tunes, raising the same cries or walking through the same streets over and over again. As it was in the morning, so it continued in the afternoon until darkness came, and with it the magical change wrought by the play of many coloured lights on the excited upturned faces ...

One of the organized bands of demonstrators which

paraded Pall Mall and Piccadilly consisted of students. They kept excellent order and sang national and patriotic songs without ceasing . . . Another procession comprised scores of butchers, most of them wearing their smocks . . . The most imposing demonstration which passed the War Office was that of the students of the Royal College of Arts. Mounted on a four-wheeled carriage, which was decorated with palm leaves, ferns and laurels was a full-sized model of the hero of Mafeking. The likeness was a striking one, and fairly took the fancy of the crowd, who joined heartily with the students when they halted outside the War Office and sang the National Anthem.

In accordance with time-honoured custom during stirring times many of the Clubs and great business houses in the West End erected gas flambeaux and devices in multi-coloured glass backed by gas flares. The devices included the Royal Arms, the national colours, and mottoes appropriate to the occasion. Soon after dusk the various gas fires, etc., were lighted up, and produced a brilliant and striking effect. Pall Mall and Piccadilly were the most brightly illuminated streets, and the former thoroughfare was almost as light as at noonday. The crowds became very dense as night advanced, and coloured fires were to be seen at frequent intervals, carried aloft by the demonstrators . . .

In the delirium of this transport the people are playing havoc with silk hats, which may be seen flying in all directions, and the curious thing is that the owners cheer as loudly as anybody else.

The Times summed up:

On Saturday the entire population of this country gave itself up to rejoicing over the relief of Mafeking with a whole-hearted zest and energy that go far to dispose of the ancient allegation that we take our pleasures sadly . . .

They were simply and frankly glad. They were hugely delighted. An occasional philosopher in a club window may have reminded himself that the relief of Mafeking really makes little difference in the course of the war, and may have hugged himself for possessing a truer sense of proportion than the people shouting and laughing outside. But he was wrong. There was no mistake of the kind he imagined. The man in the street knew perfectly well what he was shouting about. He did not suppose for a moment that he was celebrating a decisive victory, nor were his emotions of the kind that a crowning success would have called forth. In that case he would have been less effervescent and would have carried about with him a sense of responsibility which was absent from the outburst of Saturday. He was simply overjoyed because a handful of his countrymen who had fought a long and desperate fight, and whose fortunes he had been watching for months, had finally been succoured by British troops. Apart from other considerations, there was a feeling that Mafeking is an affair of the people, rather than the Army. The man in the street pictures the garrison – and quite correctly – as being largely civilians like himself, called upon to do their best and to fill the place of Regular troops. He feels a special pride in their success and a special delight in their rescue because they are representative of the race and show him the reserves of courage, energy, resource and endurance which lie away behind all the paraphernalia of the War Office.

It was stated at the start of this account that mention would be made of the night when the War Office went to bed happy. This did not occur until the following week. Monday's *Manchester Guardian* contained this note:

When the good news comes from Lord Roberts the Government Departments will hoist the flag, and take up with as free conscience the rejoicings in which the great public, careless of the difference between a news message and a despatch, has already exhausted its unauthorized emotions. The Royal Automobile Club has always had a double purpose. As stated in its first Constitution (as the Automobile Club of Great Britain) this was to be 'a Society for the Protection, Encouragement and Development of Automobilism', and 'that it should be essentially a Members Club'. In other words it is a social club with every amenity, yet one with a purpose every bit as strong as that of any political club.

Until the autocarists' 'Emancipation Day', 14 November 1896, the horseless carriage might not travel at more than four miles an hour and had to be preceded by a man with a red flag. The red flag was not always insisted upon, but the regulation was sufficiently crippling in any case. If the new type of vehicle, however well developed, might not go faster than a man can walk, it remained of less practical use than a horse and cart. Added to this, local authorities had considerable freedom in further restricting the use of cars.

Emancipation Day caused no great revolution in the magisterial or public point of view. Speed was still restricted to 12 or 14 m.p.h. and almost every man's hand and mind was still against the machines which 'barked like a dog and stank like a cat'. This was the atmosphere in which the future R.A.C. was born. Its prospects seemed about as rosy as those of a ski club in hell.

In 1898, the year following inauguration, the club joined forces with the Self-Propelled Traffic Association and became known for a while as 'The Automobile Club of Great Britain and Ireland with which is incorporated the Self-Propelled Traffic Association'. But the combined membership was only 163, hopelessly inadequate to affect either the lawmakers or general opinion.

How the club, by shows and competitions, and in 1900 by a 1000-miles trial, gradually gained adherents and developed an audible voice; how it won the King's patronage, becoming in 1907 the Royal Automobile Club, is scarcely matter for this book. (It is set out in the *R.A.C. Jubilee Book 1947*.) But how it came to take its place in the Street of Palaces certainly does matter here, and this incidentally provides a sufficient indication of the club's success in both its purposes.

The club's first premises were at 4 Whitehall Court, where it occupied four rooms. In 1902 it moved to 119 Piccadilly. These quarters were comparatively palatial. But by 1907 far more space was needed, and the Chairman began negotiations for the Pall Mall site vacated by the War Office. In 1908 and 1911 respectively the Commissioners of Woods and Forests signed agreements for the site of the club-house (86–91) and for 83–89 where the offices of the associates' department now are. Thus the R.A.C. took over all the War Office's sites with the exception of Schomberg House.

The Commissioners of Woods and Forests stipulated that the club-house must cost not less than £100,000. This was a prodigious sum for an organization which, ten years previously, had had an inventory which read: '4 call bells of which three have gone to be repaired, 3 Japanese trays, 20 tumblers . . . 48 towels, 12 dusters . . .' Yet not only did the club undertake the venture, but it built a house which cost over £250,000 – three times as much as the Reform, which in its turn had cost nearly twice as much as the Athenaeum or United Service.

The cost of the R.A.C. was naturally dependent on its great size, but nothing was spared on fittings and decoration. Because of the size of the building it was felt that, to avoid monotony, the main rooms should be decorated in different styles, British and Continental. As to the success of the building committee and their architects one can accept the judgement of the *Survey of London:*

> After Rome and Venice had provided the architectural prototypes of the great mid-nineteenth-century club-houses in Pall Mall, it seems only natural that the early twentieth century – the period of the 'Entente Cordiale' and the hotels-de-luxe of M. César Ritz – should have turned to Paris for inspiration. The Royal Automobile Club certainly enriched the stylistic galaxy of Pall Mall by adding their

substantial club-house, a polished essay in the late French Renaissance manner. This building, moreover, marked an important stage in the development of club-houses, for it contains not only the usual and traditional accommodation, but offers its members a large restaurant and recreational facilities such as the swimming-bath, Turkish baths, a gymnasium and squash courts.

Planned in the Beaux-Arts tradition, with a front to Pall Mall that owes something to Jules Hardouin Mansart (Place Vendôme) and Jacques-Ange Gabriel (Place de la Concorde), and a front to Carlton Gardens that recalls a château by le Vau or François Mansard, the club-house was designed by the internationally famous firm of Mewés and Davis (in conjunction with E. Keynes Purchase). French carvers and blacksmiths were employed to give the exterior its authentically Parisian quality.

This tribute to France serves, consciously or not, as an acknowledgement of the fact that, before the turn of the century, Frederick Simms and Harrington Moore were so impressed by the greater freedom, even encouragement, given to autocarists in France that they used the constitution of the Automobile Club de France as a model for that of Great Britain, of which they were the first organizers. And a nice return also was made to the War Office, for the most generous facilities were provided for officers during both the World Wars. It was as a direct result of this that in 1922–23 the membership rose to the fantastic peak of nearly 19,000.

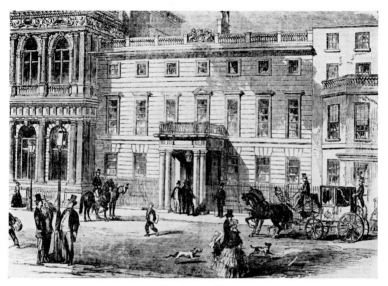

Buckingham House

Nos. 80–90, Cumberland House

23   The War Office in Pall Mall

24   A reminder of the past in Pall Mall today

15
Shopkeepers of Pall Mall

To start a shop in an expensive street is a bold venture. The owner must be prepared and able to live with the same show of prosperity for several years before he can hope for a return on what he lays out in goods, fittings, rent and rates. But hope springs eternal. Shops have a go at it anywhere, as seedlings do, and the Parable of the Sower continually proves its truth. It would be dispiriting to list all the venturers who did not find the soil of Pall Mall congenial. Most of this chapter will be concerned with those who did. They will show well enough what was needed, and that personality was almost as important as the goods offered.

Among brave failures one thinks at once of Frederick Albert Winsor trying to sell gas on the site of the Star and Garter and the Carlton Club. Admittedly this is stretching the definition of a shop, yet it is a good example of the value of personality, for in a most unlikely setting he did succeed in selling an idea which stank – for others to profit by elsewhere.

On the same site soon afterwards an attempt was made to market shoe blacking, which *is* essential to the polished life of Pall Mall. Edward Gibbon in 1769–70 lodged above a grocer's, and later 'a stinking Apothecary's'. Such shops are necessary, but the rich would send their servants to buy from them, so they might as well have been in cheaper surroundings at some distance from the home. The only justification for a shop's being in an expensive street of a fashionable district is that it offers at no more than strolling distance what the elegant and discerning would feel bound to choose for themselves.

After John Astley had divided Schomberg House into three, No. 82 became a soft furnishing and women's clothing and adornment shop, run by a succession of firms – Gregg and Lavie, William King, and R. Dyde. The last-named, between 1785 and 1796, offered the products of newly invented machines which in a single operation could print calicos in black and three colours. These made possible a much wider variety of patterns than had been known before. Dyde's chintzes made his fortune. He retired, and Harding & Co. took over.

The premises of this firm were mentioned in the account of the Duke of Wellington's funeral procession. Harding, in partnership with Howell, acquired the other two wings of Schomberg House and finally turned the whole into a department store and factory. They claimed that there existed 'no article of female attire and decoration but what may be procured in the first style of elegance and fashion' from their establishment. Upstairs were workrooms where, among much else, woollen cloth as fine as velvet was produced from the fleeces of the merino sheep in Windsor Park. King George IV when Prince of Wales ordered from Harding's chintzes for Carlton House. The firm's advertising department, with a push and go quite equal to anything at the present time, circulated every person listed in Debrett's *Peerage*, which had just been published, enclosing actual patterns of the Prince's choice. At one time almost the entire peerage were customers of Harding, Howell & Co. But the newspaper mention of their store in 1852 must be one of the last on the files. Chintzes had by then become cheap, with an almost endless variety of patterns. The firm's exclusive business declined, and the War Office took over Schomberg House, thus freeing Harding from his obligation to pull down and rebuild by 1866.

Harding was the last to venture in this field. But there had been shops for elegant ladies in Pall Mall since Gay wrote 'Shops breathe perfumes, through sashes ribbons glow'. Examples are Abraham Allen who designed and sold chintzes at No. 61, and the 'copper-plate cotton furniture for lounge, drawing room, boudoir and sleeping' of Harris, Muddy & Co. at No. 49 before the days of William Almack.

That these fashionable ladies' shops have no successors in Pall Mall cannot be put down entirely to the Industrial Revolution and the production of cheaper and still more varied materials. The reason is rather that as time went on Pall Mall and its nearby streets became less and less residential. Fewer families lived there. Men remained in the clubs and bachelors' chambers, which were often above shops. But ladies followed the fashion shops to Mayfair and Knightsbridge – or the other way round. In any case they retired from the stronghold of masculinity. Thus the field of reliable customers was reduced to men, and among men to clubmen. There were certain things that they would trust no one to buy for them – that they enjoyed buying themselves. They appreciated the precision instruments offered by the Vulliamy family which made fine clocks at 68 Pall Mall for ninety years. It was only the death of Justin Vulliamy's grandson which brought the firm to an end. (Incidentally, it was one of this family who found in his house the pall mall sticks now in the British Museum.) There is now another clock shop, Dent's, on the north side.

Books, an essentially personal choice, were in this exclusive masculine field before Jane Austen and the Brontës broke down the fence. From the age of coffee houses to that of clubs there have been booksellers in Pall Mall. Robert Dodsley's at No. 52, which Dr Johnson so often visited, has already been mentioned. Whether the Dictionary was inspired there or not, it was published in another Pall Mall house, No. 25, by Andrew Millar. When Robert Dodsley retired his brother James took his place until his lease ran out, then moved to another shop farther west along the street.

Number 81, Schomberg House, was occupied by a bookseller, Thomas Payne, and then by a nephew and his partner, 'Payne & Foss', from 1806 until Harding & Co. reoccupied the central portion, which they already owned, in 1850. Another bookseller, R. H. Evans, moved into one of Winsor's houses, No. 93, when the gas pioneer fled to France. These are only examples. There have been many bookshops in the street. There have always been gun shops, and as lately as this century an archery store. Shops for swords and fishing tackle are well established. These are all things that men would choose for themselves, taking quite as long over it as a woman does to buy a hat.

Pall Mall has always had wine to sell. The Chocolate and Coffee houses, though they specialized in what their name implies, and later sold tea, were not teetotal. They had their off-licences. When Monsieur Ozinda went back to his native land in 1724 he sold off his shop goods, which included 'Several Sorts of superfine Liquors of his own making, as Egro de Cedro, Cinnamon Water, Piercico, etc. with a Quantity of Hermitages Wine which will be lofted up by Dozens'.

The Cocoa Tree which is referred to as being in 'Pell Mell'' in the seventeenth century also had a licence for selling wine. It occupied three different houses in Pall Mall. Towards the end of the eighteenth century, when Thomas Griffiths was the licensed proprietor (his family sold wine for over half a century) the Cocoa Tree moved to No. 64, at the corner where Pall Mall meets St James's Street. This is where Rothman's showrooms now are, and before their day there was a cigar importer only a few doors off. Where there is wine to sell there is always tobacco near by.

A personal story comes to mind which stresses this important point of associations. I used to walk in the country at weekends with a dear friend now dead. On a hot summer's day at noon he would exclaim with joy at the sight of a distant church steeple. He was a good Christian, but his enthusiasm here had a different origin. He maintained that where there was a church there was a pub. Now, when one vicar serves two parishes and one publican three, that is not always true. But it was then. Wine and tobacco are similarly linked not only in poetry and song but commercial fact as well, for the connoisseur of one is generally a discerning amateur of the other. This goes a long way back. Both coffee houses and taverns provided pipes and tobacco for their customers. They also provided something to read, while for those whose taste demanded more substantial fare than newspapers there was invariably a bookshop close at hand. Thus one can trace a triple association – wine, tobacco, literature.

The Star and Garter, which survived into the nineteenth century, sold the best claret in London – according to the *Epicure's Almanack,* which surely knew. The West End taverns met a demand for quality. They were of the grade of high class restaurants, not ale houses. As for firms which are wine merchants today, St James's Street has the oldest, just twenty paces from the corner of Pall Mall. Berry Brothers have family links going back on the same site to 1699. But Pall Mall was not more than fifty years behind. In 1749 Johnson and Justerini set up shop at the opposite end of Pall Mall, at the corner with the Haymarket.

It is a romantic story. Giacomo Justerini was a young Italian very much in love with an opera singer named Margherita Bellino. When she came to England to sing at the Opera House at the bottom of the Haymarket he came too. His assets were a lot of charm, very little money and the secret formula of certain liqueurs given to him by his uncle, who was a distiller. The lady disappeared from history, but Justerini teamed up with a young man named George Johnson who had some money. They took as a place of business one of the small shops which were in the colonnade on the south front of the Opera House, facing Pall Mall. It is a nice touch that Giacomo should want to work close to the place where his lady had sung.

Partners retired and new partners took their places. The Opera House – by then called Her Majesty's Theatre – was burned down in 1867. The Carlton Hotel was built. The nineteenth century passed. The small shop, now Justerini and

Brooks, remained, royalty heading its list of distinguished clients. It was now No. 2 Pall Mall (there was no No. 1). It stood just to the east of an entrance to the hotel. Just to the west, at No. 5, was an antiquarian bookseller, Lionel Isaacs, who at the turn of the century had taken the place of another wine merchant, Page and Sandeman. Wine and literature—. In 1903 a tobacconist took over half of Isaacs's bookshop to make a very small shop indeed, which was numbered 5A. Again there was the triple association.

Louis Rothman's story is quite as romantic as that of Giacomo Justerini, perhaps more so. In 1887 he came to England in search of something more elusive than a lady's love. At the age of eighteen he had given up an assured future in his family's big tobacco factory at Kiev to seek for liberty, which did not exist under the autocracy of Russia. His chief asset was a highly trained skill, similar to the palate of a wine connoisseur. He could judge tobacco blindfold, by aroma and touch alone. He found employment in an English factory to gain experience of local trading conditions. His ambition was to make enough money to be his own master. How small was the possibility of doing so at the bottom of the ladder of the tobacco trade may be judged by the wages nearly a quarter of a century later, when the first statistics are available. In 1910 a man received 1s. 9d. for making a thousand round cigarettes and 2s. for a thousand oval ones. A quick worker could make two thousand in a day, earning 3s. 6d. or 4s.

Before he was twenty-one years old Rothman rented a single room which could serve as both factory and shop, and set up on his own. He made cigarettes at night and sold them during the day. Within a few years he was able to take a real shop in Fleet Street, where work goes on by night. He gained customers by keeping open until the small hours. Two other factors contributed to his success: though only a small shopkeeper he was an expert, able to blend exactly to the current taste and to talk about the details of his trade. He could not afford travellers or advertising, but his cigarettes were carried by journalists all over the country, abroad also, and given the surest form of advertising, personal recommendation. In 1903 he was able to move to Pall Mall. By this time he had a staff engaged in the actual manufacture of the cigarettes. But he remained the craftsman and master blender. Cigarette making was still literally manufacture, making by hand, to meet tastes which were far less uniform than they are today. His customers were interested in what he told them.

In his boyhood he had been trained in the production of the Russian-type cigarette – a long, slender card mouthpiece and a short length of tobacco separated from the mouthpiece by a wad of cotton wool. With tipped cigarettes we are getting back to that original. But many phases were passed through on the way.

Before the 1914–18 war cut off Middle East supplies and made Virginian tobacco popular, ninety per cent of Rothman's trade was in Turkish cigarettes. These were round. They were made by rolling an exactly judged quantity of tobacco in a piece of parchment shaped at one end like the nib of a pen. The nib point was inserted into an already prepared cylinder of paper and the tobacco pushed into this from the parchment roll with a wooden rod, the ragged ends being later cut off by a semi-skilled assistant. Rothman had made his name by selling his own brand of tobacco in cigarettes of a fixed size. Some of his Pall Mall customers wanted to express individuality by smoking cigarettes of unusual sizes – on the whole men large ones and women small. Here was a new test for the maker. He had learned by eye and touch to divide, say, three pounds of tobacco by a thousand to make that number of cigarettes of a fixed size. Now he had to make larger or smaller, yet still a fixed number from a fixed weight of tobacco. Occasionally he had to change from one sort to another in the course of a day.

Then came the fashion of Egyptian cigarettes. At the beginning of this century tobacco was not grown in Egypt. Egyptian cigarettes contained Turkish tobacco, but were oval in shape, because the Egyptians found these fitted better between their lips. Originally the production of oval cigarettes was achieved by preparing two boards with a series of semi-oval grooves in the surface of each. The maker made round cigarettes in the usual way, put them in the grooves of one board, placed about it the grooved surface of the other board and sat on this sandwich while he prepared the next batch of round cigarettes. Later, a method was found of cutting and creasing parchment so that the cigarettes were actually made in oval shape. This method was a trade secret, and cigarette makers from the Near East who knew it were able in England to earn an extra 3d. a thousand – until the secret got out. That oval cigarettes at that time contained exactly the same tobacco as round ones from the same maker mattered not at all. The eye of the purchaser was pleased.

The eye – or ego – of the purchaser mattered a great deal. Some individuals had their cigarette papers imprinted with their initials or family crest – or coronet if they were entitled to one. There was no difficulty about this. Others required silk or real gold or silver tips. This, though more expensive, was still not technically difficult to satisfy. But the ladies who wanted their cigarettes tipped with rose petals taxed the delicacy of the maker's fingers.

The law made it impossible to satisfy all tastes. To the man who wanted his cigarettes flavoured with menthol Rothman had to explain that no solids may be added to tobacco, and that the use of liquid essences for flavouring is very strictly controlled. He got round this particular problem by providing a cigarette case which contained a small compartment for menthol crystals, which imparted their flavour without touching the tobacco. But the pipe smoker who wanted sandalwood shavings mixed with his tobacco had to do it himself or do without.

In Edwardian days meerschaums were the thing, especially when tinted to a proper shade by smoking. There were also most improper meerschaums made in Austria. When these needed repair the owners provided the tobacconist with varying studies in psychology. Some brought the broken indecency in a case, gave their name, and were gone before it was opened. Others discussed with brazen casualness how the repair might be made. Others avoided this choice of behaviour because the delicate yet indelicate carving was covered by an innocent looking screw-on cap.

Early in this century briar pipes with a curly grain were considered best. Rothman visited a Swiss pipe-maker who had recently come to London and spent days in his cellar picking out from among thousands of half-finished bowls the small proportion in which the grain ran straight. The pipe-maker warned him that he had chosen the most unpopular type. But Rothman answered that these were the ones he wanted, and asked that they should be finished and stamped with his initials. It was not long before straight grains were considered much the best.

For the connoisseur (or he who pretends to be one) choosing a cigar inspires discussion like a wine tasting. The tobacconist who was an expert at his trade, yet unbiased in matters of taste – and who spoke with an intriguing accent – attracted those who took their pleasures seriously.

Stroll – the *Oxford Dictionary* says that the etymology of the word is doubtful. But it perfectly expresses the way of life of Pall Mall in the unhurried Edwardian days when people found much more time to appreciate the good things of the world. To lunch at the Club and then stroll across the way to buy a smoke and discuss it with the man who sells it to you. Perhaps before that to taste some port, and perhaps later on to look at books – though not at Isaacs's, for Rothman had taken over the whole shop. Even so 5 and 5A was still small. The growth was elsewhere.

16
Pall Mall Today

WE WILL END WITH a stroll down Pall Mall today and the thoughts which it arouses.

The Haymarket corner has changed out of all recognition since New Zealand House took the place of the Carlton Hotel. This new building is a shock, being so very different from anything else in the street. One thinks of the Athenaeum and the Travellers' arguing because string courses and cornices were not uniform, and here is this thing of glass soaring up three times as high as anything else. Yet it would be a mistake to dismiss it as a multi-storey greenhouse. It is excellent inside, and those outside must learn to live with such architecture. It is the work of Sir Robert Matthew, who designed the Festival Hall. Londoners of 1851 were shaken by the Crystal Palace.

New Zealand House extends to Royal Opera Arcade, having engulfed Nos. 2 and 5. Between the other side of the Arcade and Waterloo Place there has been a similar although less striking engulfment. At the beginning of the century there were nearly a dozen little shops and offices, including a printseller, a couple of wine merchants, an architect, the Sunday Society, an insurance office, and the Entertainment Reform League. Now there are only a fishing tackle shop, one small office, and an enormous bank – Lloyds, Cox & King's Branch. Sir Henry King & Co. Ltd., East India Army Agents and Bankers, was at No. 9, on the western corner of Regent Street and Pall Mall before they amalgamated with Cox's. When King's was shut officers used to bring their cheques to Louis Rothman to be cashed.

Opposite, on the southern side of Pall Mall, are the United

and the Athenaeum. The structural changes later made to the United Service were mentioned when the building of the Club was described. The Athenaeum looks almost exactly as it always did except for the addition of bedrooms on the roof. This has been the case in practically all Pall Mall's clubs and accounts for the slightly unfamiliar look of the drawings made in 1851 (facing page 96).

It may be as well to mention here the other main changes in clubs as a whole. These resulted from alteration in the rules, and the most important concerned smoking and ladies. When Edward VII was Prince of Wales he founded the Marlborough Club because he was annoyed at the restrictions on his smoking which White's imposed. Club rules have never bowed to royalty, but they have to the constant pressure by commoners, and there are now very few smokeless zones in the Clubs.

The admission of ladies almost invariably cropped up in club committee-meetings when the main item on the agenda was the more or less desperate necessity of increasing revenue. Bernard Darwin's best club story is to the point. A general meeting was discussing whether the necessary money should be found by raising the subscription or allowing some concessions to ladies. The debate threatened to be interminable until one member, who some time earlier had retired in despair, put his head round the door and said, 'Another guinea a year, gentlemen. Isn't it worth that to keep the women out?'

Ladies must not be offended. They have won a large measure of victory. And many men would not have it otherwise. Few would want clubs to hold the mystery of a lay monastery. But on the other hand if ladies do achieve equal rights in all the rooms of clubs, what will be the difference between belonging to a club and having shares in a hotel? One wants something more than a trouble-free alternative to domesticity.

As it is clubs are a unique institution. This is partly because they allow one to live above one's station. Each is a very large and very well behaved family, home for a night or a few hours in their parents' splendid house. The members are naturally entitled to speak to anyone, but don't. That clubs are full of character is proved by the fact that everybody has at least one story about them and that all these are true. My own concerns a day when I had a lot of writing to do in a short time and retired to the quietest place within reach, the chess room of my club. I had been working there alone for an hour or two when a member came in. He gave no sign of noticing me but sat down facing me across the table. I went on writing and he went on staring – not offensively at all: I just happened to be in the direction of his stare. Some time later, while my eyes read through what I had written, my fingers filled my pipe, then took out a matchbox and struck a match. Without any help from the brain they did it badly. The whole box caught alight and flared in my hand like a firework. It was very painful. The member, still without any change of expression, said quietly, 'That reminds me, I must buy some before they close'. He got up and went out.

In a hotel he would either have bothered me with attentions or pretended not to notice. In the club he showed that he noticed, even appreciated, what I had done. But if I wanted sympathy or anything else from him it was up to me to ask.

Pall Mall will become a much more ordinary street if the clubs disappear. The speculative wolves are always ready to snap up any which lag behind.

We continue to stroll westwards . . .

Numbers 9, 11 and 12 (number 10 is lost without trace) were Daniel Graham's houses in the eighteenth century. They made a Palladian-fronted group. Now No. 9, which was Sir Henry King's branch at the beginning of this century, is Williams Deacon's Bank. Nos. 11 and 12 house among other offices the Guardian Assurance Company. All the other insurance companies will not be mentioned specifically, because there are no less than twenty-seven in Pall Mall. One would not have thought that the people of Pall Mall were in such need of insurance. Perhaps it is only that insurance people feel safe there. They even have an office at No. 13. Tacked on to it, 13A, is Impossibles Limited. Crusader House comes next, built in 1892. It houses offices as it has always done.

Numbers 16 and 17, opposite the Travellers' and the Reform, were fifty-five years ago a commercial building by Sir Charles Barry. It must have been interesting to compare it with his club across the road. But it was pulled down in 1913 and replaced by a house in a kind of Renaissance style. Among many others it houses Wilkinsons, the sword people, and Dawson, the antiquarian bookseller. Offices continue to predominate until we reach the hole in the ground which is the Junior Carlton at this moment.

While walking along the sunny side of the street we have passed more buildings than there are on the other. In the same distance on the south side there are only five clubs and an office block, 'No. 100' – excluding, of course, the houses which merge into Cockspur Street and are not on the site of the pall mall alley. Now, as it was in the beginning, the houses on the south side are fewer and bigger.

Beyond the Junior Carlton is the Army and Navy, modern as 'No. 100' almost opposite, and of a different era from the R.A.C. It is the most imposing building, bar New Zealand House, on the whole north side. Beyond it to the westward there is little except offices. Still at this western end of the street the houses on the south side are better to look at. But they are not now strikingly romantic. Schomberg House is packed tight with insurance people. The ghosts of Beau Astley, Gainsborough, and Dr James Graham have no doubt been exorcised, or have left of their own accord.

Two insurance firms are in Nell Gwyn's house, No. 79. Then comes the imposing Oxford and Cambridge Club. In No. 70, which was the Guards', is the Corsetry Manufacturers Association and a bank. That No. 69 is part of the Midland Bank is more appropriate, for it was Hammersley's Bank one hundred and seventy years ago. No. 68 stands on part of the site of the Junior Naval and Military, a Victorian club which had so short a life and was so far removed from being a palace that it could not appropriately be described with the others.

In the year 1871, Nos. 66–68, the most westerly houses on Pall Mall's south side, were advertised as a building site. Tod Heatly took it at £550 a year. The Junior Naval and Military, which had been founded the year before, made an agreement with him for the erection of a club-house on the site. The club had only 270 members, but these included the Prince of Wales, the Duke of Edinburgh, Napoleon III and the Prince Imperial. So far it might appear that the Junior Naval and Military would succeed as well as any other in those High Victorian days. But difficulties immediately became apparent. The gate of Marlborough House was at that time flush with the house fronts of the south side; therefore any normal club-house would overlook the grounds of Marlborough House from the windows of its west and back walls. Possibly, since the Prince of Wales, the occupant of Marlborough House, was a member of the Club, it was thought that this might be permitted. But the Commissioners insisted that there should be no windows in these south and west walls. There could be no window in the east wall, which was against the neighbouring house. That left only the front or Pall Mall wall for admitting light. Since this faced north no sunshine would ever enter.

Yet the Club was built, at great expense. Captain John Elliott, who had obtained the lease from Tod Heatly, opened it – so far as it was possible to open it – in 1875. Within three years he was bankrupt and the club had ceased to exist. Now the site, but not the same building, houses Hambro's Bank and Walt Disney Productions Limited.

We left the north side at the Army and Navy. Although the remaining buildings are not striking there are some typical Pall Mall shops, and old associations to be remarked on. Greener's gun shop is at No. 40, a place for personal choice.

The British Legion is at No. 49 – Almack's Tavern, the first home of Brooks's, the meeting place of the Macaronis. In the middle of last century the London Library occupied it, so some of the books used in preparing this book were housed there. No. 50, which contains over twenty offices, including United States Lines, was Boodle's birthplace, the home of the Ladies' Club and Goosetree's. No. 52, another insurance office, was the site of Dodsley's bookshop, the Shakespeare Gallery, the British Institution, and later of the Marlborough Club.

We are approaching the western extremity again. Nos. 55–58, engulfed into Quadrant House, have no particular historical associations. No. 59 with its memories of the Smyrna Coffee House, is no longer there at all. Hardy Bros., the fishing-tackle people, have been at No. 61 since 1900. At No. 62 are the Dead Sea Works, at No. 63 whisky blenders, and No. 64, on the corner with St James's Street, was the last house of the Cocoa Tree Club in Pall Mall and the present West End show-room of Rothmans, the business which has expanded across Continents to become one of the world's largest tobacco concerns.

This is the western limit of Pall Mall. But it would not have been if the proposal of 1848 to carry it on to the Green Park with the Marble Arch as the culmination had been put into effect. It would not have stopped there. It would have been further elongated to Hyde Park Corner, and made a part of the trunk road to the West. Thus Pall Mall would after three centuries have taken up the task of the ancient highway it replaced. That was avoided. Pall Mall retained the dignity of comparative isolation for another hundred years. When, quite recently, it was summarily reduced to being a mere thorough-fare, this was done not by any alteration of the street plan, but the traffic flow. Pall Mall fell victim to the modern passion for the one-way street, creation of the one-track mind which holds that traffic must go faster and faster. Thus the instrument of change was Marples, not the Marble Arch.

But we must count our blessings also. Regent Street was not

carried right through to the Mall. There is still an interval where a man upon his feet can cock a dignified snook at the god who is driven by internal combustion.

It is 'really a fine-looking street with a very ill-looking western termination', wrote *The Wiltshireman* in 1845. Is that so? It has a Tudor palace at one end and Trafalgar Square just off the other. What street, taken all in all – history, architecture, pleasant associations – is richer than Pall Mall?

WORKS PRINCIPALLY CONSULTED

Anon — *London Interiors*
London   Mead 1841

ARMSTRONG, Sir Walter — *Gainsborough and his place in English Art*
London   Heinemann 1904

BESANT, Sir Walton — *London in the 18th Century*
London   Adam & Charles Black 1902
London North of the Thames
London   Adam & Charles Black 1904

CHANDLER, Dean and LUCEY, A. Douglas — *The Rise of the Gas Industry in Britain*   London
British Gas Council 1940

CUNNINGHAM, Peter — *The Story of Nell Gwyn*
London   Bullen 1903

DARWIN, Bernard — *British Clubs*
London   Collins 1943

EVELYN, John Edited by BRAY, William — *Diary and Correspondence*
London   Colburn 1950

GOWER, Lord Ronald — *Sir Joshua Reynolds*
London   Bell 1902

GRAVES, Charles — *Leather Armchairs*
London   Collins 1963

HAMILTON, J. Angus — *The Siege of Mafeking*
London   Methuen 1900

HILLES, Frederick Whiley — *The Literary Career of Sir Joshua Reynolds*   London
Cambridge University Press 1936

HOLMES, Sir Charles and COLLINS BARKER, C. H. — *The Making of the National Gallery*   London
National Gallery 1924

LAMB, Sir Walter — *The Royal Academy*
London   Bell 1951

LONDON COUNTY COUNCIL General Editor SHEPPARD, F. H. W. — *Survey of London*
Volumes 29 and 30
London   Athlone Press 1960

London Gazette	*Funeral of Duke of Wellington*
	London London Gazette
	1853
MORRIS, Helen	*Portrait of a Chef*
	London Cambridge
	University Press 1938
PEPYS, Samuel	*Diary*
Edited by BRIGHT, Mynors	London Dent 1953
ROBERTS, W.	*Memorials of Christie's*
	London Bell 1897
R.A.C. Jubilee Book	*R.A.C. Jubilee Book*
Edited by NOBLE, Dudley	London Royal Automobile
	Club 1957
TELFER, J. Buchan	*Chevalier D'Eon de Beaumont*
	London Elliot Stock 1896
WHEATLEY, Dennis	*The Seven Ages of Justerine*
	London Riddle 1948
WHITLEY, William T.	*Thomas Gainsborough*
	London Smith Elder 1915

Current Newspapers, the Rate Books, Street Directories, and the Dictionary of National Biography have also been consulted.

INDEX

A Discourse on . . . Riches
 (Polixfen), 22
Abel, Karl Friedrich, 49
Aberdeen, Lord, 102, 106
Academy, The Royal, 41, 42,
 43–4, 48, 51, 53, 81, 82, 83,
 86, 105
Adair House, 128
Ailsa, Marquess of, 111
Albemarle, 1st Duke of, *see*
 Monck
Albemarle St., 69, 101
Albert, Prince, 122
'Alhambra, Don' (*The
 Gondoliers*), 103
Allen, Abraham, 145
Almack, William, 61, 62, 69,
 70, 146
Almack's, 61, 62, 69–70, 106,
 159
Angel Court, 37
Automobile Club of Great
 Britain, *see* R.A.C.
Automobile Club, Royal, *see*
 R.A.C.
Angerstein, John Julius, 83–5
Arch, Marble, *see* Marble Arch,
 The
Army and Navy Club, The, 23,
 32, 113–4, 123, 124, 127, 129,
 157
'Arthur's', 61, 95, 102
Artists, Free Society of, 40, 41
Artists of Great Britain, Incor-
 porated Society of, 41
Artists, Society of, 40
Arts, Society of, 40
Astley, John, 71–2, 145, 157

Athanæum (Club), 78, 101,
 102–5, 106, 107, 112, 117,
 123, 125, 141, 154–5
Atomic Energy Authority, 105

Bacchanalian Dance (Poussin), 86
Bacchus and Ariadne (Titian), 86
Baden-Powell, Colonel, 135
Baker, C. H. Collins (co-author
 of *Making of the National
 Gallery, The*) 82
Banks, Mr., 66
Barclays Bank, 116
Barry, Sir Charles, 82, 107,
 109, 157
Beauclerk, James Lord, 28
Beaufort, Charles Earl of, 28,
 29
Beaumont, Sir George, 85, 87
Bed, Graham's Grand Celestial
 State, 74–6
Beggar's Opera, The (Gay), 35
Bellino, Margherita, 148
Berkeley Row, 34
Berry Bros., 148
Blomfield, Sir Reginald, 95
Blount, (author of the
 Glossographia), 6
Boer Wars, 134–40
Boodle, Edward, 70, 159
Boodle's (Club), 61, 66, 70,
 102
Boswell, James, 38, 63
Boulton & Watt, 89, 91
Boydell, Alderman John, 38–9,
 40
Boyle, Henry, *see* Carlton,
 Baron,

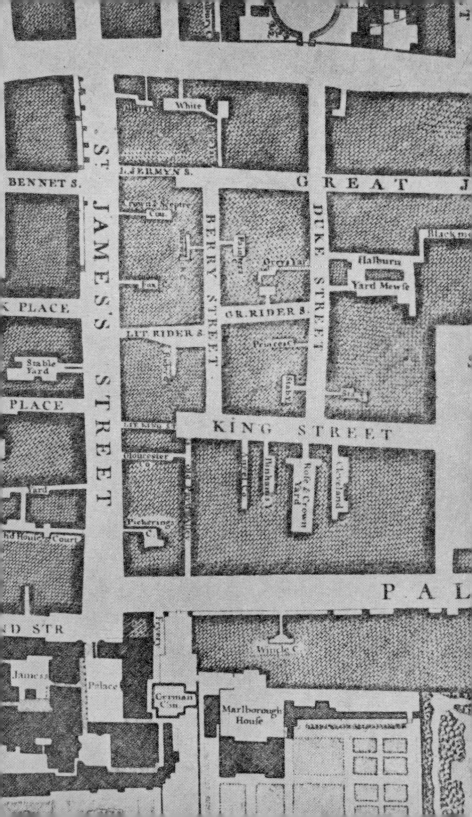